Media & Elections in Canada

MEDIA & ELECTIONS IN CANADA

Walter C. Soderlund
Walter I. Romanow
E. Donald Briggs
Ronald H. Wagenberg

University of Windsor

Holt, Rinehart and Winston of Canada, Limited
Toronto

Canadian Cataloguing in Publication Data
Main entry under title:
Media and elections in Canada

Includes index.
ISBN 0-03-921666-7

1. Mass media — Political aspects — Canada.   2. Communication in politics — Canada.   3. Electioneering — Canada.
4. Elections — Canada.   I. Soderlund, W. C. (Walter C.).

P95.82.C3M42   324.7'3'0971   C83-098641-3

Acquisitions Editor: Anthony Luengo
Developmental Editor: Brian Henderson
Design: Maher & Murtagh
Cover Photo: Arthur Herriott
Typesetting and Assembly: Compeer Typographic Services

Printed in the United States of America

1 2 3 4 5   88 87 86 85 84

Acknowledgments

Since textbooks by their very nature attempt to synthesize material for students, it is impossible for us to list here all those whose ideas and work have contributed to this book. We have consciously sought to pay our intellectual debts through the currency of footnotes, but these cannot fully express the direction given us by some outstanding scholars. One such is Professor Wilfred H. Kesterton, who has done the pioneering work on the history of journalism in Canada. The community of scholars in the communications field in Canada is relatively small, but its members have developed an admirable co-operative spirit. In this regard, we would like to mention specifically Frederick Fletcher and William Gilsdorf, with whom we worked on various aspects of the 1979 and 1980 elections. More generally we wish to thank Arthur Siegel and Edwin Black for the encouragement and constructive commentary which they have given to us at various conferences over the years.

We are indebted as well to many research assistants who helped us to record, code, clean, and process the data that appear in Chapters 3 and 4. Of this talented and dedicated group, the following deserve special mention for their large contributions: Jean Drouillard, Karen Spierkel, Len Chandler, Cindy Squires, and Colin Beckingham. We are thankful as well to the Social Science and Humanities Research Council and the President's Research Fund at the University of Windsor for making available to us the funds that allowed us to employ these people.

Books do not simply appear, but are dependent on the co-operation of professionals in the publishing field. We have been most fortunate to have worked with Anthony Luengo and Brian Henderson of Holt, Rinehart and Winston of Canada, whose talents have made the publication of this book a truly pleasurable experience. Among the many favors they have done us, their selection of reviewers of our manuscript ranks high. Frederick Fletcher, Brian Nolan, and Frank Peers gave us the benefit of their experience and insight, and we are grateful for the contribution their ideas have made to our final manuscript. During the final stages of production, Greg Ioannou, the copy editor, brought to our attention a number of infelicities of style and his work strengthened the manuscript. Among our colleagues at the University of Windsor, Kenneth Pryke, Hugh Edmunds, and Stuart Surlin have read portions of book, and likewise we are thankful for their input. Having all of this in mind, we must at this point make the usual disclaimer and accept full responsibility for whatever failings our stubbornness and poor eyesight may have forced upon the final version.

Unless a professor's scrawl is translated into something readable, manuscripts die on the foolscap. We must therefore gratefully acknowledge the contribution of the personnel of the Word Processing Centre at the University of Windsor, Roni Burleigh, Lucia Brown, Carmela Papp, Cheryl Evan, and Lyn LaPorte. Their cheerfulness in making multiple corrections in the manuscript was more than we could reasonably have expected. Finally, we wish to thank our students, who over the years provided the testing ground for many of the ideas found in this book.

W. C. Soderlund
W. I. Romanow
E. D. Briggs
R. H. Wagenberg
Windsor, Ontario
June 1983

Contents

1

An Overview of Canadian Politics and Media Development

Politics and the media in Canada have always been closely interconnected, although the nature of their relationship has changed with time. Both had their origins primarily in British models and traditions, since even the French-speaking Canadian population found the intellectual trends of continental Europe less relevent and acceptable.

In the years prior to and immediately following Confederation, the struggle for responsible and independent government was parallelled by a fight by proprietor-editors for freedom of the press and the economic viability of their publications. While these fundamental battles were relatively quickly won, partly because they had previously been fought by the British and to some extent the Americans, the linkage between the development of the press and the political system remained strong.

At no time is this relationship more obvious or more important than during elections. Elections are keystones of our democratic system, providing consummate opportunities for the media to function both as conduits for the messages of political parties to the electorate and, perhaps more importantly, as independent influences on the political process. Does one of these functions predominate over the other? Are the media passive conveyers of the gospels politicians choose to preach or are they independent proselytizers for paths to social and political salvation? Do media organizations adopt a consistent role from one election to another, or do they change according to circumstances? If it is the latter, what are the relevant circumstances? Are all types of media similar in these respects?

These are some of the questions this book attempts to answer. In order to provide a context for the analytical chapters to come it is useful to briefly review the principal periods of media and political development in Canada.

The Pre-Confederation Period

W. H. Kesterton and Paul Rutherford, among others, have given us admirable accounts of the beginnings of media development in Canada.[1] These demonstrate that the colonial newspaper, from the time the first appeared in Halifax in 1752 until Confederation or even the 1880s, was heavily dependent on political patronage and government support. The earliest publications were little more than government mouthpieces, established primarily to inform the small literate elite about official proclamations, Empire and foreign news, and such matters as shipping movements. Governors like John Graves Simcoe considered printers indispensable for such purposes,[2] and editors, at least those who were even marginally successful, almost invariably doubled as King's Printers. Those who lost that position, as one Anthony Henry did in Nova Scotia in 1766, soon ceased to publish unless some other branch of the local establishment provided the necessary support. In Henry's case, the Nova Scotia *Chronicle and Weekly Advertiser,* which he founded as an independent journal, survived less than one year.[3]

As a result of this dependency, the characteristic journal of the second half of the eighteenth century was "a pallid, neutral, harmless sheet without any really vital role to play in the social and political life of the community."[4] While even the earliest publishers paid lip service to the idea of freedom of the press, due mainly to libertarian ideas current in British intellectual circles, reality was quite different. In British North America the prevailing philosophy could most correctly be described as authoritarian. The elite not only were confident that they had a natural right to rule, but also believed that they possessed the concomitant right to manage political opinion through control of the press. At the time, there was no significant challenge to this state of affairs. Newspapermen occasionally kicked over the traces, but for the most part they appear to have accepted with few qualms a position of loyal support for King and Empire and the appointed representatives thereof. Undoubtedly personal economic survival dictated such a stance, but there is little evidence to suggest that the early gentlemen of the press had much desire to publish contentious political material in any case.

This bleak picture began to change early in the 1800s. Indeed, the first half of the nineteenth century was a period of ferment that gave birth, not without difficulty, to fundamentally new political ideas. Because these struck directly at authoritarian thinking, they were as significant for the developing press as for the machinery and processes of government itself. Those decades saw the slow and painful emergence of the concept of responsible government.

Presupposing as it did an executive answerable to and dependent on the confidence of a body of popularly elected representatives, responsible government implied revolutionary changes in the social and political role to be played by the masses. At the same time, it provided not only grist for the toiling presses but also legitimization for their increased outspokenness. The period saw the emergence of what Rutherford has called the *opinionated press*. Certainly a notable number of newspaper editors began to voice vigorous and even strident criticisms of government sins in the early years of the nineteenth century, and their numbers increased as time and the political debate wore on. Even those to whom political change was anathema were drawn into battle. By the 1830s most of the more important journals could be classified as either Reform or anti-Reform (that is, Liberal or Tory) though some, of course, attempted to tread the middle ground.[5]

The challenges that newly confident and self-reliant editors increasingly threw out to officialdom with respect to what could be published, and who should decide what was publishable, met with stout and only slowly weakening resistance. Numerous editors, especially in the early decades of the century, suffered prosecution, imprisonment, the destruction of their business premises, and even physical attacks when they offended conservative sensitivities. One who did so, Henry Winton of the St. John's *Ledger,* had both his ears cut off with a clasp knife when he was set upon by hoodlums on a dark night. Moreover, an employee suffered the same fate only a short time later. Official investigations produced no clue as to the perpetrator of these barbarities.

As late as 1835 Joseph Howe was charged with "seditiously contriving, devising and intending to stir up and incite discontent and sedition among His Majesty's subjects" for publishing in his *Novascotian* a letter that accused magistrates and police of corrupt practices. Significantly, this was precisely 100 years after Peter Zenger had won a precedent-setting victory when he was brought up on a similar charge in New York.[6] Howe, too, was victorious, with a jury verdict in his favor delivered in direct defiance of the Chief Justice's explicit instructions. But while it was a major step toward freedom of the press, one obstacle remained: the continuing necessity for papers to rely on political subventions in order to escape bankruptcy.

A great many did not escape this fate. Down to the closing decades of the century it was easy to begin a newspaper, and a host of them came and went with meteoric speed if less brilliance. For instance, more than 20 were founded in London, Ontario, between 1830 and 1867, but only four survived to celebrate the birth of the new Dominion. The ability to read and write, a few hundred dollars, and some second-hand equipment were enough to make one an editor and publisher, but not enough to sustain one long in that position.[7] As in the pioneer press period a century earlier, the easiest way to ensure survival was to obtain the Queen's Printership. This was worth, claimed George Brown, $26-27,000 "even in a bad year" for work that had a value of no more than $10,000.[8] Failing that, some other connection with political, religious (mainly in Lower Canada), or, rarely, business patrons might suffice. But without a patron of some kind, enterprise and hard work were seldom sufficient to continue in the newspaper profession.

The need was not entirely one-sided. If journals needed political support, politicians needed journalistic exposure, especially in light of the increased importance that responsible government conferred on the public at large. Politicians frequently decided that the only way to ensure that their views were adequately placed before the public was to become newspaper proprietors themselves, or the indispensable patrons of appropriately needy organs. Many politicians became pressmen for these reasons, and, vice versa, many editors were drawn into the political realm by their partisan press activities. Of these, George Brown of the *Globe,* J.B.E. Dorion of *Le Defricheur,* and Edward Whelan of the Charlottetown *Examiner* are among the best known of the owner/ editors, but many others, including John A. Macdonald, George Cartier, Leonard Tilly, and Charles Tupper could also count on support from a pliant newspaper.

Macdonald, for example, appears to have carried on a lengthy correspondence with Brown Chamberlin of the Montreal *Gazette* during the 1850s. These letters make plain not only the kind of service that was expected of the hired pen, but also illustrate one of the many mechanisms that were used to pay for it. On February 2, 1855 Macdonald wrote that:

> Your article in the *Gazette* was on the whole favorable, but I wish you had
> come out a little stronger.... We expect from our friends a generous
> confidence and hope that when you have anything to our disadvantage
> you will communicate with us, and hear our answers and explanations
> before committing yourself or your paper against us. In fact we want you to
> 'Be to our faults a little blind/And to our virtues always kind'.... We are
> making arrangements about the Government patronage in the way of
> advertisements, which we will complete in a few days, and will advise you
> thereof.[9]

As has been pointed out elsewhere, "the party in office was expected to release a stream of money to its press friends.... By 1862 the Conservative Government of the two Canadas was spending well over $100,000 per year to feed an ever-hungry gaggle of proprietors."[10]

These transactions were always conducted "in confidence." We would for instance know none of the details of Macdonald's dealings with the *Gazette* had not Chamberlin disobeyed explicit instructions to destroy the correspondence. Yet when pushed, even the most distinguished colonial journalists defended the patronage practices and denied inconsistency between their client status and their claims to independence. George Sheppard at one time declared that in bowing to the collective wisdom of his party the journalist was only doing his duty. Although as far as we know George Brown never articulated such a view, he certainly behaved throughout a long public and journalistic career as if he accepted it without question.[11] The Montreal *Gazette* in 1858 maintained that the independence of a paper was not compromised by serving a particular party out of "sincere convictions."[12] Shortly afterwards, the Montreal *Pilot,* owned by Queen's Printer Rollo Campbell, put a more honest case:

> Now, supposing for the sake of argument, that the *Pilot* is what the *Globe*
> describes it to be — the 'hired organ' of the Government, we ask in the
> name of common sense, why should it not?... If Mr. George Brown keeps

up a newspaper, and hires men to advocate his particular political views, and defend them when attacked by his adversaries — why should not Mr. Macdonald, or Mr. Cartier, or Mr. anybody else?... We esteem it as a cause for honour rather than shame to be recognized as an organ, ready and able and willing to defend the Ministry against the baseless attacks of the *Globe* or any of the smaller fry who do as that paper tells them.[13]

Explanations, justifications, and protests notwithstanding, the *opinionated press* of the early 1800s had by the time of Confederation become the *party press*, and such genuine independence as might have gleamed briefly through the earlier authoritarian gloom had again been effectively dimmed.

Confederation and Beyond

In *The Life and Times of Confederation* Peter Waite has provided a vivid portrait of the interplay between journalistic and political forces during the birth of the new Dominion. He argues that "for those who believed in Confederation the newspapers were not only useful, they were indispensable."[14] They were just as indispensable to those who considered Confederation a scheme suddenly hatched by madmen, or, worse, conceived to cure ills from which the spokesman's locale did not suffer. A large and active array of papers (in 1865 there were 380 that published weekly or more often)[15] witnessed and participated in the Canadian birth process, from the seduction at Charlottetown, through the gestation period in Quebec, to the delivery at London. While some assumed the role of midwives, as many sought to be abortionists.

However, all saw the issue of union in terms of local interests, thus demonstrating the "separate worlds" that historian Arthur Lower has suggested the British North American colonies lived in at the time of Confederation.[16] Several papers, like the Saint John *News* and Montreal's *La Minerve,* found themselves boosting union because they saw their respective cities becoming commercial or industrial capitals of the enlarged state. Such organs as the Halifax *Chronicle* and the Montreal *Herald,* on the other hand, worried that Confederation would bring either economic hardship or less prosperity than might be achieved through, for example, closer economic co-operation with the United States. Others were less specifically mercenary, but were nonetheless fearful or optimistic on the basis of anticipated post-Confederation effects on local conditions.[17] The first Dominion Day, July 1, 1867, was greeted with outpourings of thanks to Divine and Royal providence on the one hand, and something approaching cynical despair on the other. As *La Minerve* wrote:

Et post finem annorum faederabuntur (Dan.XI,6). [And at the end of years they shall join themselves together!] In associating these words of the Holy Ghost with the legitimate hope expressed yesterday by all our mouths and hearts we do no more than give a new impetus to the glorious aspirations it is our right to entertain. Yesterday, two solemn voices, the carillon of the

bells and the roar of the cannon, hailed the birth of a new power and, fresh
and smiling, the young Queen of North America came to the throne that
love and patriotism had erected for her. Sublime moment when a generous
nation, from whose bosom springs youth and life, breaks the bonds that
fettered its infancy and asserts itself with confidence before the peoples of
the world.[18]

In contrast, the Yarmouth *Tribune* was ironically bitter:

Five years hence, every child will be born into the world with a thorough
knowledge of reading, writing, arithmetic, geography, history, classics
and the Spencer rifle drill.... A Canadian will discover the North Pole, and
a contract will be issued to bring it south and mount it on the Parliament
Buildings at Ottawa, and the Yankees will bow down to it reverently
morning and night....Every householder will have a couple of oil wells in
his cellar and a gold mine in his back garden...There will be...no
temperance societies...no Fenians...no bribery at elections...no
policemen, no lawyers...no *Globe* newspaper...no railroad...no doctors,
no national debt. Everybody will be contented and happy and Canada will
be a paradise on earth.[19]

The early decades of the fledgling Canadian nation would not, of course,
bear out the raptures of the victorious Confederationists or the cynicism
of their deflated opponents. It is a testament to the pragmatic realism of
the former colonial inhabitants, and to the shrewd political leadership
of John A. Macdonald, that in a remarkably short time the press and
politicians were united in the cause of nation-building. The conception
of the child might have been a mistake; carrying it to term might have
been an even greater error; but now that it had seen the light of day it
was everybody's duty to see that it grew to lusty adulthood. Some
adjustments in the basic design were necessary: the terms under which
Nova Scotia entered the federation, for instance, had to be altered to soothe
the continuing sense of grievance felt in that province. Thus mollified,
Joseph Howe, the loudest and most capable of the Nova Scotian anti-
Confederationists, had been enfolded into the central cabinet within six
years of Dominion Day. Moreover, Prince Edward Island, which, like
Newfoundland, had declined the initial opportunity of union, had
rejoined the family.

As an issue for passionate debate, Confederation quickly faded away,
temporarily taking with it other celebrated political causes like representation by population and the French-English juxtaposition. Replacing
these as topics of central interest were strategies for nation-building,
railways and the corruption accompanying their construction, and
ethnic/religious issues like those aroused by Manitoba school legislation
and the Riel Rebellion. These were matters into which any newspaper
publisher could happily sink his teeth, but they more closely related to
day-to-day concerns than to fundamental principles of political life such
as were inherent in the earlier responsible government, representation
by population, freedom of the press and Confederation debates. It was a
period in which government could concentrate on the minutiae of

consolidating gains already achieved and the press could cheer, boo, and direct from the periphery.

Confederation did not mean the end of the party press. But almost before the ink was dry on the British North America Act, a combination of social and technological developments began a transformation that would eventually produce a continent-wide network of genuinely free and independent journals. Little more than ten years after Confederation, the out-going president of the Canadian Press Association could claim:

> In another important respect the press of Canada has made remarkable progress. It has, we may say, nearly altogether got from under the control of the politician. We mean by this, that a paper now-a-days very rarely and to a very small extent, depends for its existence or support on any individual or party....Scarcely one can now be found who is mean enough to go round hat in hand begging for support, or who will so debase the profession as to play sycophant to some political magnate for a few dollars.[20]

Government advertising, he went on to explain, had come to be largely a business arrangement, rather than the means of "bolstering up a weakly sheet," and newspapermen had adopted a healthy business tone and dependence on "enterprise, perseverance, and fair business competition" to produce their "due share of public support."

These views in 1878 were undoubtedly more prophetic than descriptive. Throughout the 1870s and 1880s the Liberal and Conservative parties continued to establish journalistic spokesmen for themselves, to the extent that "the 1880s probably marked the high point of party journalism in Canada."[21] But thanks to the 1866 discovery of how to make paper cheaply from wood pulp, the gradual perfection of movable type and power presses, the growth and increased literacy of the population, and the creation of several new provinces from the western territories by 1905, the press could also be said to have entered its Golden Age around the turn of the century. A continuing appetite for politics and the scarcity of competing news and entertainment sources ensured a market for a steadily increasing press output. One authority has suggested that Canadians' fascination with politics in the late nineteenth century can be compared to their devotion to hockey in the second half of the twentieth.[22] Certainly the number of journals increased dramatically during the late 1800s. Between 1864 and 1900 the number of newspapers in Canada more than quadrupled, and within this total, daily papers increased by a factor of more than five, from 23 to 121. Even as early as 1881 there were 61 dailies and 413 weeklies across the country.[23]

Greatly increased publishing costs, attributable mainly to the cost of sophisticated new machinery and the wages of the staff necessary to operate it, forced proprietors to become more businesslike and competitive. Nonetheless most expected that loyal party service would not go unrewarded. Many party papers by the eighties were owned by consortia of wealthy partisans, and operated with an eye to electoral more than to financial success. Others were also assisted by advertising expenditures, job printing contracts, and the purchase of subscriptions. For instance, between 1883 and 1888, the two major Toronto dailies, the Tory

Mail and the Liberal *Globe,* received $10,030 and $109 respectively for federal government advertising. Between 1896 and 1900 a magical reversal occurred, coincident with the change of government, and the *Globe's* revenue from the same source blossomed to $9,623 while that of the *Mail* dwindled to $917.[24] As late as 1905 the Laurier government actually printed a confidential booklet headed "a list of newspapers authorized to receive Government patronage."[25] *Globe* editor John Willison could aptly point out to publisher Clifford Sifton in 1901: "I think I could prove to you that within the last five years between three and four hundred thousand dollars of party money, or what amounts to party money, has been put into Liberal papers in Canada."[26]

Substantial changes in the style and content of papers and to some extent in their relationship with political sponsors did occur in the last 20 years of the 1800s. The chief agent of these changes was (as described by Rutherford) the *people's journalism,* which by the early 1880s began to challenge the pre-eminence of the party press. People's journals, examples of which are the *Star* (1869) and *La Presse* (1884) of Montreal, the *News (1881), the Telegram* (1876), and the *World* (1880) of Toronto, the *Journal* (1885) of Ottawa, and the *Herald* (1889) of Hamilton, were founded on the premise that subservience to party had made a mockery of freedom of the press and had produced organs that served only the politicians and their upper-class friends. "An independent press desires above all things the good of its country for which it denies itself the temporary benefits which partisanship gives" proclaimed the Montreal *Star* on July 5, 1882. A year later (September 29, 1883) the Toronto *News* vigorously explained its *raison d'être* by cataloguing the sins of the party papers: "the public mind has been debauched, the properties of life outraged, the self-respect of voters ruined, and the Parliament of Canada made the stamping ground of monied adventurers and political sharks."[27] What was needed was a press that was a public educator, a tribune of the people, a voice of justice, and a fount of wisdom, all of it coming in a package and at a price the common man could afford.

The price was a simple matter: people's journals sold, almost without exception, for one cent, compared to three (occasionally two) cents for the party papers. They were simply and directly written, employed more colorful language, and were more innovative in their use of illustrations, headlines, and story titles than their rivals. Content changes were even more important that the stylistic ones. News rather than comment was the main thrust of the new journals. The editorial, though usually surviving in a shortened form, became just one among the many features aimed at different sectors of the population. Foreign news, especially that dealing with wars and other crises, was an inevitable component, but the people's journals also carried a good deal of commercial and financial information, reprints of novels, even the sermons of popular divines, and ran specials designed to appeal to women, working men, or youth. Above all, they turned a spotlight onto *local* affairs. They were sensationalist, with "the human interest story, crime and police reports, social scandal, 'scoops' and 'crusades,'" and publicity stunts being prominent hallmarks of their operation.[28]

For our purpose, the most significant changes related to political coverage. While the people's journals generally kept correspondents in Ottawa, their reports of parliamentary speeches, or, for that matter, constituency speeches, were reduced to a fraction of the space devoted to them in the party press — and not infrequently eliminated altogether. The people's editors did not abstain from politics; they simply attacked the establishment on the one hand and championed the cause of the masses on the other. The party system and machine politicians were denounced as responsible for social ills, which included everything from corruption and mismanagement to the apathy of the public. Big business — the railway and utility companies in particular — was also a favorite, and related, target. Political and business leaders were frequently portrayed as the joint perpetrators of a cynical and self-serving neglect of the respectable, productive, hardworking, underprivileged working man. Thus E.E. Sheppard, the radical editor of the Toronto *News*, in 1883 launched a crusade for the introduction of the republican system and the extension of the elective principle to all branches of government. As well, several papers carried on campaigns for manhood suffrage, while others concentrated on advocating a tax system that would reduce the burden on the common man.[29]

That the people's journals "mirrored the passions, prejudices, and moods of their own readers" was the mark of their success and their failure.[30] Apart from the amorphous, ritualistic demand for social justice, they had in common only a rebellious energy and tone. No coherent ideology, which might have made the people's papers into a new political force, ever emerged. Given that they printed a fair share of jingoism, imperialism and, worst of all, religious and ethnic bigotry, that is probably just as well.

For all their shortcomings they were unquestionably instruments of democracy in that they opened the political process to a significantly larger proportion of the population. Their enthusiasms, reckless as some of them were, broadened the range of political debate far beyond what the party organs would have introduced, and they made independent political criticism and advocacy at least acceptable if not respectable.

The people's papers were a temporary phenomenon. As each paper became financially successful, or made a last-ditch effort to avoid bankruptcy, it usually came to sup with one political devil or the other. By the mid-nineties few had escaped either a Conservative or a Liberal label.

Yet the party press, in engulfing the people's journals, took on many of their characteristics. Some people's papers were successful, which showed that there was a market for their kind of journalism, and for the airing of their kind of issues. The party press, if it were to compete for readers and advertisers, would have to adapt accordingly. And adapt it did, more successfully in English than in French Canada, until, by the turn of the century, the old-style elite journal of opinion had been almost entirely replaced by a new mass journal of diversified content. If party ties were as pervasive as they had been prior to Confederation, they were less constricting, and could no longer be considered the first and most important necessity for journalistic success. The party press had been challenged and most newspapers were not longer automatically at the politicians' disposal.

The Era of the Mass Circulation Daily, 1900-1930

From the vantage point of Canada's second century it is sometimes difficult to remember that 1867 marked the beginning of the climb to independent statehood, not its achievement. The British North America Act united four hitherto separate colonies under a single name and a government more or less free to pursue domestic interests. Mutual effusions about the Birth-of-a-New-Nation-Destined-for-Greatness notwithstanding, neither British nor Canadian political elites at Confederation, or for most of the nineteenth century, ever considered the heretical notion that any change had occurred or should occur in Canada's status as part of the British Empire. Such matters as foreign policy could not, many supposed, properly be decided on the banks of the Ottawa.

More than a few impertinent Canadian heretics emerged before the new century was past its infancy. French-speaking Canadians, of course, were never celebrants of the glories of Empire, but it was more gradually that their English counterparts began to chafe at the quasi-independent limbo in which Canada appeared to be caught. At the outbreak of the Boer War in 1899 most English Canadians were still exuberant in their support for the British cause and ready to assist in its pursuit. However, as a succession of other issues relating to imperial defence, international representation, and treaty-making powers came to the fore, the lack of Canadian autonomy quickly became a paramount political theme, as first responsible government and then Confederation had been in earlier periods.[31] As before, the press had a role to play in these concerns, though it would change considerably by the time the gloom of the Great Depression settled over the country.

The early twentieth century newspaper was truly Canada's first mass medium. As early as 1903 it could be said, with only a touch of exaggeration, that the aim of the newspaper was "to be all things to all people." Not long thereafter, the press was "fast on the way to becoming a standardized product like the other consumer goodies produced by the industrial machine."[32] At the same time newspapers were experiencing vigorous and healthy growth. As Kesterton's data indicate, Canada boasted more newspapers in 1913 than before or after that date.[33]

This was to a large extent both natural and inevitable. The twentieth century dawned with bright expectations of commercial and industrial greatness ahead. The mere fact that the promise was there and Canadians were already enjoying a richer and more varied way of life meant that the political process and the day-to-day rhetoric of politicians had a less constant and universal public appeal. Politics was simply no longer the only game in town. The newspapers, in diversifying their content to appeal to a mass readership, reflected and intensified that development, especially after post-World War I financial troubles forced the demise of some 40 dailies and ignited among the survivors greatly heightened concern for profits.

In the years leading up to World War I, however, Canadian autonomy — what the term did and should mean, and how it could best be secured or protected — was heatedly debated by the press in the context of a series of proposals and occurrences. First came the Boer War, quickly followed by Joseph Chamberlain's proposal to create centralized machinery for imperial defence purposes. Other events included the Alaska Boundary Award (1903) and various arguments about who should sign international agreements in Canada's name (for instance, in 1907). Most significantly, the controversies over reciprocity — that is, continental free trade with the US — and Canadian contributions to the Royal Navy (1910-11) became major election issues in 1911. Although they approved of Canadian participation in the Boer War and later advocated reciprocity, Laurier and the Liberals stood for asserting Canadian independence wherever feasible and reasonable. The Conservatives, while in principle also supporting greater autonomy, were inclined to see it in terms of partnership in the Empire and to see Liberal policies as containing the risk of American domination, if not annexation.

On the whole, newspapers in the early years were loyal to their party's line, though some went beyond what the leaders were prepared to endorse. The French-language press, for instance, generally adopted a position that was little short of isolationist. Many English-language papers in turn sounded a Loyalist trumpet louder by far than did the Tory leadership itself.

It was not, however, a clear-cut debate between Nationalists and Loyalists, or between English and French, but a strange cross-cutting mixture of the two. English-speaking Tories and, more significantly, a good many English-speaking Liberals were more than a little suspicious that French-Canadian attitudes not only betrayed a lack of appreciation of the Empire but also demonstrated a lukewarm devotion to Canada. These suspicions went largely unspoken until World War I broke out, when there was near universal agreement that the debate on autonomy should be put aside for the war's duration. The majority of the French as well as the English press applauded Canada's entry into the war without much concern regarding its causes. The major exception was Henri Bourassa's *Le Devoir,* which opposed Canadian involvement under any circumstances. Bourassa found he had almost no sympathy among his compatriots, but his outspoken views were enough to bring harsh condemnation from such journals as the Toronto *News* and Toronto *Telegram* and to some extent the *Globe.* None of those publications hesitated to generalize from a sample of one; Bourassa might be the worst of his kind, but that was certainly no reason to be complacent about the rest. Indeed, they suggested that his position proved beyond doubt that such insidious aspirations as bilingualism and French-language schools outside Quebec were little short of the "national outrages" an Ontario cabinet minister labelled them.[34] Not even as great a liberal and nationalist as John W. Dafoe of the Manitoba *Free Press* could bring himself to support bilingualism. There could, he thought, be no possible common denominator of nationality in Canada other than the English language, and hence schools outside of Quebec itself should remain firmly English and secular.[35]

Matters would get worse before they got better. In retrospect it is surprising that Canada survived the 1917 union government and conscription crises without civil war. These emotion-filled controversies pitted English against French, regardless of party lines, more completely than ever before or since. The idea of forming a union government composed of the best brains from both parties originally came from Liberal sources — especially the Manitoba *Free Press* and the Toronto *Star*. Most union advocates also approved conscription, so Laurier, who opposed it, felt that he could not then support union government. Papers like the *Free Press* broke ranks with the Liberal party, in effect supporting Borden and the Conservatives, while in Quebec papers like *Le Croix* and *La Liberté* issued the first calls for secession and/or revolution, and mobs attacked the business premises and homes of those who were of a different political persuasion. Sadly, the press in this instance was a long way from being a positive force for national unity.

Yet in some sense the excesses of the war years were a cathartic last fling. Papers that made it through war-time inflation (newsprint in 1921 was nearly three times as costly as it had been at the beginning of the conflict) into the twenties slipped into sober introspection if not docility. The international and domestic battles of the previous decade had been enervating in more ways than one, and the time had come to count one's blessings, take stock of one's achievements, and chart a sound commercial course for the future — both nationally and journalistically.

While issues like Canadian autonomy and differing French-English viewpoints would not be forgotten overnight, they could and should be consigned to the rhetorical back-burner. To do otherwise was to risk offending some portion of the population, and offending people was not the way to sell newspapers. Moreover, the events of 1917 had effectively disposed of the need to toe the party line. The new watchword was "objectivity," with news columns that were impartial and even political reporting that was now rarely cast in a partisan mould. The birth in 1917 of Canadian Press (CP) as a co-operative news service added a further tone of neutrality in political matters to participating and subscribing newspapers.

According to Paul Rutherford, newspapers in the post-World War I period "popularized an entrepreneurial idea that glorified the businessman as a national hero, acquisition as a public good, and competition as a progressive force."[36] Unflattering as these judgments may be, they reflect a political and press environment that was an improvement on the shrill divisiveness that had prevailed during the war.

From a Single Medium to a Multimedia Society

Canada's first mass medium, the newspaper, was virtually without competition until the early 1930s, by which time it was mature in the sense that it was regarded as an important and serious-minded institution. As with all adulthood one could applaud the arrival of sobriety and restraint while harboring a twinge of nostalgia for the youthful vitality and passion they replaced. For those who found relinquishing the latter qualities altogether too painful to bear, there was an alternative: abandon print communication altogether and embrace instead a rapidly growing infant, radio, which had begun to intrude into Canadian life. The progression was from a relatively simple communications system, politically relevant to a small attentive public, to a complex, technologically sophisticated series of systems with the potential for much wider influence.

Radio broadcasting as we know it began on the North American continent in the 1920s. In Canada, a Marconi station was first licensed as a commercial operation in Montreal with the call letters of XWA (later CFCF).[37] Radio, while started in Montreal, developed almost simultaneously in the 1920s across the country. From its inception radio was a cultural, and hence a political, football. Politicians did not immediately recognize radio's potential; indeed, the fact that licensing of would-be broadcasters was initially entrusted to the Department of Marine and Fisheries, under the assumption that it should be viewed as an extension of marine services, is an indication of how little it was at first understood.

But mere toy though it might have been, it was fantastically popular, and it ran into two immediate problems that necessitated government interference in its operations. First, Canadian stations had great difficulty competing with stronger American stations broadcasting on the same wavelengths, in the absence of agreements on the allocation of exclusive spectrum usage. Second, there was already concern before the twenties had ended that fledgling Canadian radio was becoming the instrument for the transmission of American culture. In arguments that were to be repeated by later generations of Canadians, it was maintained that most Canadian stations carried popular American programs because it was easier and less expensive to do that than it was to produce domestic content.[38]

The Aird Commission, which submitted its report in 1929, indicated that Canadians preferred Canadian broadcasting. While the statement was ambiguous, in that Canadians have always shown a preference for broadcasting content originating in the United States, the Commission's conviction was clear: "the destiny of Canada depends upon our ability and willingness to control and utilize our own internal communications for Canadian purposes."[39] One of the recommendations of the report resulted in the creation of the Canadian Radio Broadcasting Commission and later, in 1936, in the creation of the Canadian Broadcasting Corporation.

This is not the place to review in detail the operations of the CBC or to recount the transformations through which it has been put in more than 50 years by the various committees, commissions, and ministries that have pried into its workings. These are reviewed in Chapter 5. What should be noted here is that radio brought a new dimension to the traditional relationship between politicians and the media. Politicians' interest in the press had always been narrow and selfish. Newspapers were use-

ful as personal and party mouthpieces, as tools in the perpetual propaganda contests that constituted politics, but publishing in the collective
sense was not thought of as essential to the national interest. Radio, on
the contrary, from the time of the Aird Commission Report, was considered a sort of national resource to be managed in such a way as to provide a protective shield against foreign (i.e., American) cultural intrusion.
The strength of this resolve was certainly not constant over the years. At
times, in fact, it was almost nonexistent. The resolve did survive and by
the time television appeared in the early 1950s, it found expression in
any discussion about the role of the media, including the printed press.

One-third of all Canadian homes had some sort of radio receiving device by 1930. In urban centres it was more like half. The unending
gloom of the Great Depression served to reinforce the attractiveness of
technology's magic to such an extent that neither bread lines nor dust
storms could prevent 75 percent of households acquiring radios by the
time economic recovery was in sight. Politicians could hardly avoid concluding that radio presented an ideal means of reaching more people
faster than ever before.

Yet there was no stampede to politicize the microphones and there
were no attempts to develop a party radio. One reason for the latter was
the fact that many of the private radio stations were owned by press bar-
ons who were disinclined to resurrect a practice that print journalism
had only recently escaped. Another and more practical reason was that
partisanship might discourage advertisers even more quickly in radio
than in newspapers. In any case, radio remained unsullied by party labels.
It was used for electoral campaigning, on a local and regional basis, during the late 1920s, and, with some initial trepidation, for federal
campaigns. Both Prime Minister Mackenzie King and Opposition Leader
R.B. Bennett utilized it to attempt to reach nation-wide audiences, though
with undetermined effect as far as impact on the voters was concerned.

It was President Franklin Roosevelt who was to demonstrate how effective radio could be for political communication. His famous fire-side
chats over coast-to-coast radio in the United States came to characterize
the Depression as surely as unemployment, but with the opposite effect.
The talks were a soothing ointment applied by a kindly parent to the
hurts of millions and, as time would tell, they paid handsome dividends
in the form of electoral success.

In Canada, those dark days also served to heighten realizations of radio's
potential. In Alberta, William (Bible Bill) Aberhart had already discovered that the air waves were ideal carriers for the evangelical messages
of the Calgary Prophetic Bible Institute. When, in 1932, he decided that
the spiritual salvation offered by Christianity had to be supplemented
by the material salvation promised by Social Credit, it was naturally radio that transmitted the Good News. Aberhart was a master performer
before a microphone. His voice ranging up and down the octaves, he
thundered and cajoled and pleaded with his listeners to have faith in
Christ and Major Douglas (the Social Credit theorist) in about equal
proportions. He found his way into almost every Alberta home on a regular
basis and he was accepted in the vast majority of them for the same rea-

son that Roosevelt's chats were welcomed by Americans — and many Canadians. Here was a voice of hope, of understanding, of deliverance when none seemed to be likely from any other quarter. Social Credit swept to power in the Alberta election of 1935 and maintained a stranglehold on that province until 1971. Much of the thanks (or blame) could be laid at radio's door. At least, as John H. Irving has put it, "It may be doubted if there could have been a Social Credit movement without Aberhart's use of the radio."[40]

Aberhart was not the only Canadian politician who found radio an effective propaganda instrument. While the successes were not of the same magnitude as experienced in Alberta, the political broadcasting experience in neighboring Saskatchewan was very similar. There, a young Socialist Baptist minister, T. C. Douglas, found similar success for the fledgling Co-operative Commonwealth Federation (CCF) through his radio broadcasting orations in the early 1940s. In Quebec the newly organized Union Nationale under Maurice Duplessis used radio as the principal avenue for attacking the entrenched Liberal regime of Louis Taschereau in 1935 and 1936. Again the offensive succeeded and forty years of Liberal rule came to an end. On the other hand, when R. B. Bennett's desperate Conservative Government tried to recover from the threat of defeat in the federal election of 1935 by resorting to a series of broadcasts in the form of dramatized political discussions critical of the Liberals and Mackenzie King, they were nevertheless swept from power.

By itself radio certainly did not ensure electoral victory, but it conferred an advantage on those who took the trouble to master the techniques of using it. The political careers of those who possessed such skills were considerably enhanced. To ensure that party radio did not arise and some equity in broadcasting opportunities was guaranteed to all political parties, a 1939 White Paper on political broadcasting recommended that all parties represented in Parliament should have free broadcast time during elections. This first occurred in the 1940 campaign and was made a permanent feature of Canadian broadcasting in 1944. The free time, which was proportional to each party's numerical strength in the House of Commons, could be supplemented by as much paid advertising as a party could afford.

The traditional press did not fold its type and slink into the underbrush with the appearance of radio. Publishers were understandably nervous for a time, mainly about radio's impact on advertising revenues. They sermonized frequently on the desirability of a pure, commercial-free CBC system on the British model, and when that battle was lost in 1938, "they ranted and raved, throwing a tantrum inspired by a sense of betrayal and some fear."[41] But the tantrum was mitigated by the fact that many publishers were by that time deeply involved in radio ownership themselves, and, in any case, newspaper operations did not seem to have been significantly affected. Profits were scarcely high during the Depression, and the number of dailies declined to a low of 87 by 1945. But radio listening did not seem to be a substitute for newspaper reading. There were several reasons for this. Radio was perceived to be an entertainment medium and the most popular listening periods were early afternoon and evening hours. Moreover, the new medium generated new advertisers rather than enticing the old ones to shift from print to voice. Traditional publishing thus was little altered by the coming of radio. It appears, however, that publishers gradually adopted a more serious demeanor, as befitted the senior communication medium now that the frivolities could safely be left to the newcomer to provide. Both newspapers and radio faithfully recorded events, including political comings and goings, on a day-to-day basis, but more as observers from afar than as partisan participants.

Post-1930 Canada was not without its political problems, of course. The 1930s began auspiciously with passage of the Statute of Westminster by the British Parliament. Apart from authority to amend the British North America Act, specifically omitted at Canada's request because no agreement could be reached on an acceptable amending procedure, the Statute removed all previous limits on the autonomy of Canada and the other Dominions.

The long search for full independence was over, but at the time that accomplishment seemed a good deal less tangible than the widespread distress caused by the Depression. The inability of the municipal and provincial authorities to cope adequately with the calamities it engendered led eventually to the appointment of the Rowell-Sirois Commission to look into federal-provincial financial relations. The Commission called for the broadening of federal responsibilities relative to those of the provinces and the readjustment of the financial arrangements between the two levels of government. With the exception, however, of the transfer of constitutional responsibility for unemployment insurance, these recommendations were unfulfilled.

World War II, however, enhanced tendencies toward federal centralization, as populace and economy alike were mobilized in a single-minded pursuit of allied war aims. The one discordant note during the war was sounded by the second conscription crisis, which occurred in 1944. Prime Minister Mackenzie King had pledged himself and his party not to introduce conscription, but two years into the war it became apparent that voluntary enlistment would not be adequate to fulfil the nation's military manpower needs. French-Canadian attitudes toward conscription had not altered appreciably since 1917. King resorted to a plebiscite on the question and, not surprisingly, the English majority prevailed. Quebec was scarcely pleased with the result, but its reaction was less violent than on the earlier occasion, and King was able to emerge without significant loss of support in the province.

Thousands of casualties and millions of dollars in wasted resources notwithstanding, Canada emerged from World War II with economic strength, international prestige, and a transcendent central government. The last of these set the scene for the gradually developing conflict between the federal and provincial levels of government, which has been the outstanding characteristic of recent Canadian political life, and which one authority could by 1980 call ''the crisis of the Canadian federal system.''[42] That crisis has been fuelled by the escalating complexities of national and international economic and social interdependence. It has been exacerbated by, and has helped to kindle, separatist inclinations in Quebec and widespread discontent in western Canada. Consequently, national unity, or the lack of it, has become a frequently mentioned theme in Canadian politics.

Communication systems became more complex and all-encompassing as these difficulties developed. With the beginning of television broadcasting in 1952 one could say that the multimedia era had truly arrived. From the point of view of those already in the marketplace, however, the danger was that television would be the ultimate medium all by itself. It did, after all, combine the best features of radio and the movies; it had a public acceptance that made the earlier reception of radio seem lukewarm; and, as time proved, it appeared capable of unending improvement and expansion.

By 1960 most of the older media were in desperate straits. Movie attendance had fallen by 50 percent; radio was almost totally eclipsed; and advertising had fled from even the giants of the consumer magazine industry to such an extent that the only choice appeared to be between immediate and lingering death. Newspapers, however, again demonstrated their basic resilience. They were not totally unaffected by television's savage rampage. They too lost advertising dollars, as older people were found to prefer to receive news via television rather than expend the greater effort that newspaper reading required. Newspaper circulation, which had climbed more or less continuously for more than two hundred years, continued to increase, although the rate of growth slowed perceptibly. Newspaper publishers had less cause for alarm than most of their media cousins.[43]

Television was not very innovative in its early days. Televised newscasts, for example, consisted mainly of on-camera readers, supplemented by still photographs of events, and occasionally by filmed footage. But this was a classic case of the whole that was greater than the sum of its parts. Television had impact. It had the immediacy movie newsreels lacked; it could briefly convey a good deal more information than a newspaper headline; and, of course, its visual dimension brought events into everyone's living room with a reality that not even the most dramatic radio reader could match. Television could convey messages that affected viewers on both the cognitive and affective levels. These need not be wholly consistent with one another. Verbal accounts of an event might, for instance, be objectively phrased and dispassionately rendered, but the pictorial accompaniment might well make a far stronger statement, or, in the extreme case, serve to make quite a different impression than the carefully modulated words. Pictures indeed tended to speak louder than words, and the possibility of conscious or unconscious pictorial bias, present in the media to some extent since newspapers began publishing photos in the late nineteenth century, was now far greater.

It has not been incidents of visual distortion that have troubled the relationship between politicians and television or other media personnel. Political events continue to be a major focus of attention for all media, and politicians have learned to play to the television cameras before all else. Strangely, political leaders unanimously declined the offer of free-time telecasts during the 1953 federal election, but since then practically everything has come to be framed with an eye to the 30-second television newsclip. Great efforts are devoted to staging "media (i.e., TV) events" that will display the party leader or other prominent figure in what is hoped will be a favorable light. A premium is put on a good television image and on the ability to package and market that image.

Since the coming of television (the federal campaigns of 1957 and 1958 were the first in which television was extensively used) politicians have courted the media more assiduously than ever before, but have rarely been able to establish an easy relationship with them. Federal and provincial leaders have complained that their treatment by the media has been unfair. Prime Minister Trudeau has probably given voice to such complaints more frequently than most of his predecessors or contemporaries, though John Diefenbaker in the last years of his prime ministership could also scathe journalists bitterly, and even Lester Pearson was known to grumble at the attitudes of the gentlemen of the press. The most general complaint has been that the media are too critical, that they concentrate on trying to embarrass and emphasize the negative aspects of practically everything.

Some evidence suggests that the media have at last become what journalists have long aspired to be: a genuinely independent Fourth Estate. The media that were hard hit by the television tidal wave in the fifties have managed to reclaim a sufficient portion of the public's attention to remain viable and profitable. Each now appears to occupy a more or less comfortable niche. A live-and-let-live philosophy and a degree of mutual support have come about (it is now not unusual to see radio advertise on television, and in turn promote television programing).

The media generally have acquired a self-confidence bordering on brashness. While they must operate within the confines of actual and threatened government controls, and the CBC must still rely on public money, the media need no longer depend on partisan favors or fear displeasure from any political source. The occasional denunciations by prime ministers are not only tolerable, but may be interpreted as evidence that a self-assigned role of public watchdog is being adequately fulfilled.

Whether that is the proper role for the mass media, whether it is being carried out in an objective or a self-serving fashion, and especially whether the role is conducive to national unity or tends to encourage parochial and regional separatism are questions that will be addressed in the following pages.

Notes

[1] W. H. Kesterton, *A History of Journalism in Canada* (Toronto: McClelland and Stewart, 1967), and Paul Rutherford, *The Making of the Canadian Media* (Toronto: McGraw-Hill Ryerson, 1978).

[2] Rutherford, p. 2.

[3] Rutherford, p. 6; Kesterton, p. 4.

[4] Kesterton, p. 9.

[5] Ibid., pp. 12-18.

[6] See Kesterton, p. 21 for details of the Joseph Howe trial and the dismissal of the charges against him. In the United States, because of his attacks in the New York *Weekly Journal* upon the colonial bureaucracy for incompetence, Zenger was charged in November 1734 with raising sedition. See Edwin Emery, *The Press in America*, 3rd. ed. (Englewood Cliffs, N.J.: Prentice-Hall, 1972), pp. 57-66.

[7] Rutherford, pp. 9-11.

[8] Robert Hill, ''A Note on Newspaper Patronage in Canada during the late 1850s and early 1860s,'' *Canadian Historical Review*, XLIX (1968), p. 48.

[9] Hill, p. 47.

[10] Rutherford, p. 28.

[11] Ibid.

[12] Hill, pp. 47-8.

[13] Ibid.

[14] P. B. Waite, *The Life and Times of Confederation: Politics, Newspapers, and the Union of British North America* (Toronto: University of Toronto Press, 1967), p. 17.

[15] Ibid., p. 6.

[16] Arthur R. M. Lower, *Colony to Nation: A History of Canada* (Toronto: McClelland and Stewart, 1977), p. 103.

[17] Rutherford, p. 32.

[18] Kesteron, p. 40.

[19] Ibid., pp. 41-2.

[20] *A History of Canadian Journalism*, I (Toronto: Canadian Press Association, 1908), pp. 89-90.

[21] Rutherford, p. 49.

[22] Ibid., p. 34.

[23] Kesterton, p. 39.

[24] Norman Ward, ''The Press and the Patronage: An Exploratory Operation,'' in J. H. Aitchison, ed., *The Political Process in Canada* (Toronto: University of Toronto Press, 1963), p. 9.

[25] Ibid., pp. 9-10.

[26] Ibid., p. 7.

[27] The passages from the Montreal *Star* and the Toronto *News* are cited by P.F.W. Rutherford in ''The People's Press: The Emergence of the New Journalism in Canada, 1869-99,'' *Canadian Historical Review*, LVI (1975), p. 174.

[28] Ibid., p. 178.

[29] Ibid., pp. 189-91.

[30]Ibid., p. 184.

[31]See Kesterton, pp. 177-8.

[32]W. D. Lesueur, "The Newspaper Press and the University," *Journalism and the University* (Toronto: Queen's Quarterly, 1903), p. 255; cited in Rutherford, *The Making of Canadian Media*, p. 52.

[33]Kesterton, p. 71.

[34]Ibid., p. 185.

[35]See M. G. Donnelly, "The Political Ideas of J. W. Dafoe," in Aitchison, p. 109.

[36]Rutherford, *The Making of Canadian Media*, p. 74.

[37]A concise history of Canada's early broadcasting system is contained in *The Canadian Broadcasting Corporation: A Brief History* (Ottawa: Canadian Broadcasting Corporation, 1976), pp. 1-2.

[38]Ibid.

[39]*Report of the Royal Commission on Radio Broadcasting 1929* (Ottawa: The King's Printer, 1929), pp. 12, 13.

[40]"Interpretations of the Social Credit Movement," in Hugh Thorburn, ed., *Party Politics in Canada* (Toronto: Prentice-Hall, 1963), p. 92.

[41]Rutherford, *The Making of Canadian Media*, p. 83.

[42]Richard Simeon, "Some Suggestions for Improving Intergovernmental Relations," in Paul Fox, ed., *Politics: Canada*, 5th ed. (Toronto: McGraw-Hill Ryerson, 1982), p. 98.

[43]For a discussion of newspaper circulation development in Canada, see *Royal Commission on Newspapers* (Ottawa: Minister of Supply and Services Canada, 1981), pp. 63-6.

2

Thinking about Communication

We live in an information society. Our media systems inform, advise, and instruct us about our environment and about changes that affect our future. For entertainment, for information about the necessities of everyday life, and to expand our horizons, Canadians turn primarily to the media.

This is also true in the political world. Political hopefuls depend on the media to reach the voters in election campaigns. Once in office, their activities, and those of the appointed officials they direct, are publicized daily through the media. Citizen attitudes reach politicians through the same conduit. In the future, two-way interactive systems may revolutionize this communication, but will not alter its essential importance to political life. Whether such a technological advance would lead to greater citizen control of government or the reverse is a matter of debate, but that its impact would be significant is not. It is clear that both modern democracies and totalitarian systems are founded on the ability to disseminate information to large numbers of people.

This chapter presents an overview of the information society, reviews some of the theoretical underpinnings of our media systems, and probes the application of that knowledge to elections in the United States, where most of that work has been done, and in Canada. Finally, the chapter outlines the research design and methodology used to gather empirical data on media behavior in the 1979 and 1980 Canadian federal election campaigns.

The Information Society

More information is moving faster, reaching more people, travelling greater distances, and being carried by more complex media systems than ever before. Moreover, these trends are accelerating as time and space limitations are overcome by developing technology. More people are employed in dispensing information, and there is an increasingly conscious attempt to understand information dissemination processes. These changes affect the hardware to receive information and the capacity to transmit it, and perhaps alter the need for literacy as we know it.

We spend more time than in the past attending to media as observers, listeners, and readers. It is estimated that the mass media audience around the world is growing in numbers and expanding in terms of territory, and that "almost everyone will be in the audience in a matter of decades."[1] Between 1950 and 1975, these international growth rates were: press — number of copies, daily newspapers — +77%; books — number of titles per year — +111%; radio — number of receivers — +417%; television — number of receivers — +3235%.[2] The ready and increasing availability of media hardware — often through discount merchandising — has tended to remove any "media technology mystique." There is little mystery today about the operation of television or about storage-retrieval information systems. Today, information storage and retrieval hardware is becoming an increasingly common household item, as prices are reduced in this highly competitive industry. Also, educators have adopted media technology to the extent that audiovisual library learning is common, even at the elementary school level.

Satellite systems have revolutionized the sending of information. Their capacity to carry multiple information signals (audio and video) and their fixed costs irrespective of distance have made moving information from one location on the globe to another more economical. Figure 2-1 illustrates how transmitting information to any location within a satellite footprint will cost the same, regardless of the distance involved.

Figure 2-1
Satellite Rebroadcasting

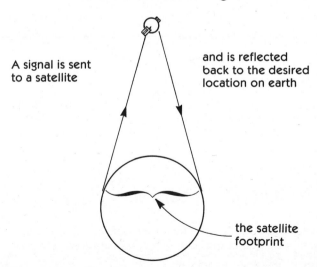

A signal is sent
to a satellite

and is reflected
back to the desired
location on earth

the satellite
footprint

Advances in broadcasting engineering have resulted in a considerably expanded number of frequencies for radio and television broadcasting. Consequently, frequencies are no longer a scarce resource, and the control that continues to be exercised over them is based on policy as much as on technical considerations. In addition, the capability of cable television systems to provide more channels creates the potential to satisfy the viewing needs and tastes of almost everyone.

Clearly these technological advances have had an impact on the political system and its practitioners. Almost instantaneous comment from political figures can be demanded by the electronic media, which may well lead to a degree of spontaneity—some might say greater honesty—from those involved in the political process. This would be true at least for those who have not become skilled in the evasive rhetorical techniques demanded by the new situation. There is another side to these developments, however, on which pessimists might focus. Those who govern, or would like to, now have at their disposal a much more sophisticated process with which to persuade the public.

Some discussion of literacy is essential in this examination of an information society, and the discussion is particularly relevant to the overall theme of this book—the relationship between the mass media and political processes. How can anyone meaningfully participate in the politics of one's society without possessing the skills to comprehend political messages or the capability of commenting on these messages? It has frequently been pointed out, for example, that in traditional societies where few possess basic reading and writing skills, the level of political participation also tends to be low.

Diverse criteria have been used to measure illiteracy. If an everyday task such as addressing an envelope is the standard, then according to a Ford Foundation study released in 1979 as many as sixty-four million adults in the United States may may be classed as illiterate.[3] Other tests, taken at different times and places, produce quite different results. The UNESCO standard of literacy is the ability to read and write a short simple sentence on everyday life.[4] By this criterion approximately 40% of the world's population over the age of fifteen may be considered illiterate.[5] The Director-General of UNESCO indicated in 1981 that the number of illiterates in the world would probably reach a thousand million persons before the end of this century, if current trends are maintained.[6] UNESCO also estimates that about 60% of world illiterates are women, and that the number of female illiterates is increasing more rapidly than the number of male illiterates.[7]

Are the traditional skills of reading and writing necessarily prerequisite to active participation in the political process of a society, as they once were? Studies consistently demonstrate that we tend to spend less of our daily lives in practising traditional literacy skills than we do with mass media information systems, which clearly do not reflect traditional literacy skills.

In fact, mass media systems are rapidly developing their own grammatical-rhetorical forms of expression, which, incidently, we have all become accustomed to using and understanding. Marshall McLuhan's

insistence that "the medium is the message" comes to mind when looking for some definition of such newly developing forms. While it is necessary to express caution about any attempt to interpret McLuhanisms,
in this instance McLuhan was articulating what every mass media prac-
titioner learns very early in working at the trade, that is, that form gives
meaning to content by complementing it or contradicting it, but always
by shaping it. A front page headline, for example, is in fact saying, "This
is the most important story in today's newspaper," in addition to whatever words appear in that headline. In a fairly traditional newspaper, a
headline banner on the front page may indeed be saying, "Because we
rarely use banner headlines, this story is unusually important."

In television and film, the "grammar" of mobility (panning, dollying,
and zooming, for example), editing, and pictorial design are all tricks of
the trade. Research is beginning to consistently confirm that such factors as changes of camera angle and shots selected by news editors affect
the retention of information as well as perceptions of messages.[8]

In another field, those who design highway information systems are
increasingly lowering their demands for traditional literacy skills by in-
troducing a new symbolic language that is understood by all who drive
cars. For example, during the last decade signs that earlier stated DO
NOT PARK FROM HERE TO THE CORNER have been replaced with signs
that utilize a capital P with an oblique stroke through it and a horizontal
arrow. Thus such a sign says exactly what the digital sign said, perhaps
with more impact, and perhaps for more persons.

Audiovisual expressions, which characterize media hardware systems,
convey information in a way that is not consistent with cognitive learning,
but rather with the affective domain of learning. The information from
our mass media is understood because it is felt and not only absorbed
through the cognitive processes. This learning presents less of a challenge than that associated with the traditional school system. There,
because of the reading and writing requirement, the reward of information is not as immediate as is the case with television.[9] Thus, the rapid
application of media systems to education around the globe can be readily understood. It should be pointed out, however, that such applications may, in fact, be counterproductive, if our concerns are with the
development of traditional literacy skills. But that they are effective in
imparting information to more people, with less effort on their part, is
no longer questioned. For example, the availability of miniaturized, tran-
sistorized radios in societies within which traditional literacy has been
very limited has revolutionized mass communication. Radio has, in effect,
become the global town crier.

This extensive review of media literacy underlines one important
conclusion: the mass media are well suited to the transmission of impressions or images, and less suited to transmission of linear logic. In
the area of political activity, we are increasingly exposed to *image
candidacy*, with concomitant diminishing emphasis on substantive
issues. Principles of product marketing are now used to design election
campaigns. This has been the case in Canada since the election of 1962,
when, in emulation of Kennedy's successful tactics in the US presiden-

tial campaign two years earlier, advertising agencies and pollsters became a prominent and permanent feature of electoral politics.

A growing percentage of the labor force is involved in the production and dissemination of information. Among the burgeoning group of information specialists are those who produce, sell, and distribute information: teachers, journalists and other media practitioners, information processors, and librarians, as well as those who function in information infrastructures, such as VDT and word processor operators and telecommunication workers. Of the total labor force in the United States, 53.5% are information-task oriented.[10] Because of the similarity in the industralization patterns of the United States and Canada, and because of the close ownership links between US and Canadian industries, similar trends characterize the Canadian labor force.

In these circumstances it is little wonder that in recent decades governments and international organizations alike have become very concerned with the information society from a public policy viewpoint. A UNESCO report released in 1981, for instance, emphasizes the importance of examining communication systems and utilizing them for the benefit of world societies. One of the report's 82 recommendations calls for the creation of a world broadcasting system which would transmit the message of the UN more effectively to all peoples of the earth. The chairman of the commission which prepared the report urged, ''that the UN should establish a broadcasting system of its own that would broadcast 24 hours round the clock in not less than 30 different languages.''[11]

While UNESCO may be seeking to create a global village, those who run national governments are more concerned with preserving their national identities. Karl Deutsch, for instance, equates a national state with an information system existing among a particular group of people.[12] Governments object to the distribution of information that may destabilize their political systems. The Russians jam Radio Free Europe, and while Canada has not yet begun to jam NBC, CBS, and ABC, it has adopted media regulations that present a defensive posture against the intrusion of information from the United States because it is perceived to undermine Canadian culture.

Theoretical Framework

To understand mass media interactions with political processes, some familiarity with communication theories and models is essential. Canadians, it should be noted, have contributed significantly to these theories, especially Harold Innis and Marshall McLuhan. On the technical side, Canadians have also assisted with the development of such innovations as satellite transmission and interactive television-computer systems. But technical developments in communications occur within an international context, and communications theorists, however important their individual contributions, must also be considered within that wider community. Perhaps not surprisingly, it is necessary to reach far into the past to unearth the beginnings of the study of communications.

The Beginnings

People have always been fascinated by the subject of communications, from earliest recorded history. These early concerns focused on individual expression and its influence on society. Rhetoric (speech-craft), as it was called, was associated with poetry, ethics, the law, and politics,[13] and classical theorists have bequeathed to us concepts and principles which are still being explored. Probably the single most concise, explicit, and enduring collection of these principles is to be found in Aristotle's *Rhetoric*, which continues to be regarded as the seminal work in the literature of speech-craft.[14] The *Rhetoric* is remarkable in that it contains concepts concerning the processes of persuasion which are apparent in the media of today. Advertising and public relations activites, public campaigns of any kind, and perhaps electoral campaigns in particular, rest on ideas explored centuries ago by Aristotle. Very few modern election tactics are entirely unanticipated by designs to be found in the *Rhetoric*.

Modern Developments

The development of modern social sciences, coincident with the popularization of media, generated research focusing on man in the environment — an environment that we have discussed above as an information society.

Around the turn of the century, an increasing concern, born out of philosophy, about people's relations with each other and with social structures spawned social sciences organized into disciplines including anthropology, psychology, and sociology. More recently, economics and political science, and most recently, journalism-communication studies developed. Inevitably these new disciplines concerned themselves with relationships between people and mass media, because media function as society's information system. While earlier research activities had, in different disciplines, sometimes touched upon the mass media, in the 1940s and 1950s we find mass media and communication research beginning to coalesce under an umbrella that today is labelled Communication Studies. What these disciplines have in common is the investigation of information processes in modern society.

Although the study of media and communication processes is accurately considered an interdisciplinary activity, more and more of this activity is becoming unified into a common body of knowledge. Hence it is claimed that under the broad rubric of communication studies, a discipline exists in its own right. Some scholars hesitate to accept that proposition, noting that the body of research knowledge resides within several disciplines and does not constitute a firm and formal set of methodologies and assertions that might be called media-communication theory. Nonetheless, a body of knowledge regarding communication phenomena does exist, and its multi-disciplinary nature can be appreciated by reviewing the parts of an act of communication.

Many models designed to help us understand the communications process have been developed. Among these, Harold Lasswell's contribution, published in 1948, is of seminal importance.[15] His paradigm is, simply "Who says What in Which medium to Whom and with What effect." It is diagrammed in Figure 2-2.

Figure 2-2
A Basic Communication Act

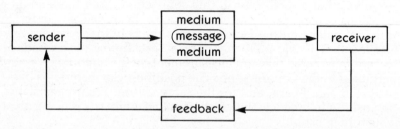

By examining each part of this figure, we are able to get an overview of contemporary concepts and concerns about communication processes.

1. Who
In our diagram the "who" is the sender or initiator in a communication system. Research focuses on the sender in a variety of ways. Psychologists for decades have been examining senders as individuals and have concentrated on motives for initiating messages. Sociologists study the relationship between various groups of senders and their social context. Journalism and communications researchers examine mass media organizations as senders. Among others, those with public policy orientations are concerned with the regulation of senders, whether it be by controlling individuals through libel and slander laws, or organizations by specifying conditions of ownership. Governments themselves, of course, communicate through Royal Commissions and legislative committees in order to affect legislation. Political scientists probe the behavior of political actors in a number of different areas: those with a public policy orientation are concerned with the regulation of senders, while students of political behavior are interested in the messages that both mass and elite political actors send to each other, and international relations scholars are interested in how states communicate a variety of messages to international society.

2. What
The message itself ("what") attracts the concern of several disciplines. Consideration of the substance of the message, its meaning, its style, and its form has inspired students of language and journalism-communication. Message content, because it is easily accessible, has attracted a good deal of attention. Newspapers, for example, are available in their original printed form or on microfilm, and historians have capitalized on this source of contemporary comment on the events they are studying.

Those with quantitative methods training have used content analysis, while others have relied on more impressionistic techniques. Content such as propaganda, especially in wartime, is a field of study in itself. Since audio and video recording techniques have become generally available, the analysis of content no longer needs to be confined to the print media. Moreover, the more artistic forms of expression such as films, novels, plays, and even songs may also be studied in this manner. It has long been realized, however, that it is not only the words or pictures themselves that are relevant in this connection. Both the amount and the location of content may be of significance. In journalism, for instance, space is a major limiting factor, just as time is in the broadcast media. The allocation of column inches of print, or minutes and seconds of air time, are considered relevant measurements of the importance accorded a particular item of information. The positioning of material is likewise considered significant, and for the same reason. Front page status, or lead position in broadcasting, indicates that emphasis is being given to the item in question.

3. Which Medium

In the study of the media, research divides into two broad areas, interpersonal communication and mass communication. Students of interpersonal communication focus on vocal expression and body language (facial expression, gestures, posture, dress, and general demeanor) as media of communication. Mass communications research concentrates on the characteristics of media hardware. For instance, media technology has occasioned research that probes the different capacities of media to select and distribute information. The same information transmitted by different media will have a different impact on receivers. The difference may be just a nuance or it may be very major. These differences are at the heart of research given impetus by Harold Innis (technological determinism) and Marshall McLuhan (the medium is the message).

Television, for instance, has the obvious capacity to add a dimension that is lacking in radio or print communication: the visual. Therefore, while the content of the transmitted message may be essentially the same, the visual element added by television (or, to a lesser extent, a newspaper photograph) may influence the way in which the information is evaluated. In the 1960 televised debate between Nixon and Kennedy, Nixon's appearance, his heavy beard, facial expressions, and body movements made a strong impact on viewers and served to lessen his appeal relative to his opponent. Had radio been the only medium available for this debate, the overall evaluation of the two candidates might have been quite different.

4. To Whom

The receivers of information have been probed from diverse research perspectives. Media systems and/or their content, in fact, are sometimes considered to prosper or fail according to the active preferences of receivers. Thus, measurement of receivers' exposure to and perceptions of content comprise a large part of what is known as audience or market studies. In democratic societies, recognition of the importance of receivers as holders of opinions has led to the widespread use of "advocacy advertising" in a deliberate attempt to create public opinion favorable to government policy.

5. What Effect

Messages are sent to cause a reaction in a receiver. Political messages are usually intended to alter or reinforce opinions, attitudes, beliefs, or behavior. The receiver's response completes the act of communication, but is at the same time the first step in another communication process. Senders of messages observe the response of the receiver, and subsequent messages, or lack of them, are based on that response. Does willingness to continue viewing, reading, or listening constitute a response or feedback? Those who gather circulation figures or listening and viewing ratings seem to think so, but others might consider that feedback implies some activity on the part of the receiver, like writing a letter to the editor or calling a radio talk show. Whatever the case, there is little doubt that feedback has become a concept of considerable interest.

In an international context, the effects of media information have been studied by UNESCO. Third World societies are increasingly concerned that they are in danger of being socialized into the lifestyles of First World nations, who control sources of information and information distribution agencies. Such fears eventually led UNESCO to establish, in 1977, a commission to study these issues with a view to creating a "more just and more efficient world information and communication order."[16]

While communicators and scholars of communication alike agree that messages have some cumulative effects on receivers, they are far less certain precisely what this is or how it comes about. Without doubt, this is the most difficult aspect of communication research, and the one in which the much work remains to be done.

Our discussion of the five elements in Lasswell's paradigm is obviously not exhaustive. As with any model, the attempt to present a simple explanation of a system masks many complexities, both in the parts of the model and in their interrelationship. It is for this reason that the search for knowledge grows into mountains of literature. Though the Lasswellian paradigm represents a useful first step in understanding communication phenomena, at least some of the other voluminous writings on communication must also be briefly explored here.

Theories of Communication

Early thinking about the communication process concluded that the basic communication act was an overt transfer of information (in literal or symbolic form) from one locale to another. There was a source clearly identified as a sender and another as a receiver. In effect, it was suggested that it was a process in which someone was doing something to someone else, such as changing the latter's attitudes or behavior in a unidimensional manner.

In large part, such early designs of the communication process accompanied developing studies of propaganda, which were associated with major military conflicts of the twentieth century. However, given such protracted periods of study as provided by "hot" and "cold" wars, theories about communication matured rapidly. Such maturation occurred because of contributions by scholars working in a wide variety of disciplines. Theorists began to conclude that communication was neither a simple thought transference, nor could it produce a predictable response. It was, rather, a sharing of mutually understood cultural symbols. Further, the greater the volume of the mutually understood symbols in the dialogue between persons, the more effective would be the communication process between those persons.

Such general agreement about the essence of the communication process has, in itself, given an impetus to studies about propaganda and persuasion — particularly in the light of rapidly developing technologies.

Once technology provided the means to distribute increased numbers of symbols at great speed over wide distances, it became imperative to refine and expand the understanding of these general principles. Theories of communication of various sorts accordingly proliferated.

Probably the whole panorama of such theories is relevant to the political process in one way or another. There are some excellent overviews of these theories,[17] but only the four which provide the most appropriate frameworks for discussing the mass media in elections will be reviewed here. They fall into two groups of two. The first group, comprised of concepts of "selective perception" and "uses and gratifications," addresses the question of how receivers respond to the mass media information reaching them. The second group, "gatekeeping" and "agenda-setting," attempts to explain how media content is extracted from the social environment and prepared by senders for public consumption.

Selective Perception

Theorists have used the concept of selective perception to describe how we respond to content. Simply stated, we select media content from what is available to us, and we choose to interpret that information according to our predispositions, by what we want to perceive or have habitually perceived.[18] In the political context, the electorate selects and interprets information that is or is perceived as being favorable to one's parties, candidates, and issues. The information selected, in other words, will usually be determined at least in part by the receiver's psychological needs and wants.

While they are normally included under the rubric of selective perception, two associated concepts are occasionally studied as separate theories. *Selective exposure* is the conscious or unconscious tendency to structure our environment so as to avoid information that is at variance with strongly held views or obversely to seek information which reinforces strongly held views.[19] Research about *selective retention* suggests that we are inclined to remember information with which we are sympathetic, and are likely not to retain information with which we have little or no sympathy.[20]

Uses and Gratifications

The uses and gratifications approach examines the reasons individuals select particular mass media and content within those media. While researchers of mass media content usage may not have constructed a theory of communication, they have adopted an approach to the study of how individuals select and respond to content.[21] Studies using this approach believe that people have particular uses for media content (i.e., information or entertainment) and receive particular gratifications from that content. Thus, while this may be an oversimplification of a large accumulation of knowledge, individuals search media content in what has been broadly described as a "systems maintenance" activity, which involves seeking assistance in interpreting events, and perhaps seeking guidance for behavior and reinforcement for attitudes and values.[22] This approach assumes that audiences actively search for self-defined gratifications from media content.

Gatekeeping and Agenda-Setting

The two theories of *gatekeeping* and *agenda-setting* concern themselves with media content from the perspective of the sender rather than that of the receiver. In this sense, they focus on how content is selected from the social environment and the consequences of that selection process.

Gatekeeping and agenda-setting are so interrelated that they can be considered together. Gatekeeping is the process of information selection by decision-makers in the media (reporters, editors, publishers, etc.), while agenda-setting is essentially the cumulative result of gatekeeping processes. This relationship is shown in Figure 2-3.

Figure 2-3 is a schematic representation of the processes involved between the occurrence of an event somewhere in the world and the response of an individual to it. Depending on the location and charac-

Figure 2-3
The Relationship between Gatekeeping
and Agenda-Setting

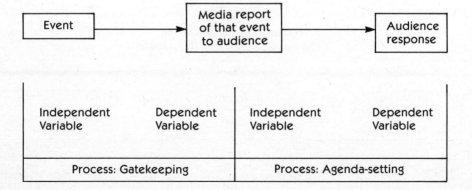

teristics of that event, various mass media channels provide crucial links between it and how it is eventually perceived, if indeed it is presented to the mass public at all. This process may be broken down into two parts. First, there is the process intervening between the occurrence and the media report of that event, where the event serves as the independent variable and the media output the dependent variable. Then there follows the process intervening between the media report of the event and the audience response to it, wherein the media output is the independent variable and audience response is the dependent variable. The first of these processes will be examined under the general rubric of gatekeeping, while the second will be considered within the framework of agenda-setting.

Wilbur Schramm, in his 1960 article, "The Gatekeeper, A Memorandum," provides an explanation of how a news story might move from "India to Indiana."[23] From Schramm's ideas, we have derived the following news flow, which identifies specific gatekeepers along the way, in this case the movement of news from Windsor, England to Windsor, Ontario.

The point where the information moves from one source to a receiver may be considered as a point where information "passes through" a gate or, as in this instance, every person in the communication chain. There are two characteristics of the gatekeeping process: first, the gatekeeper (reporter or editor) controls the volume of information that passes through the gate if, indeed, any passes through at all; second, the information that passes through the gate is likely to take on the characteristics of the gate through which it passes. For example, two editors working independently with the same information are likely to select somewhat dif-

Figure 2-4
New Flows and Gatekeepers

The person who sees the
news happen in Windsor, England

The Canadian CBC reporter who talks to this news source

Transmission via satellite to
Canadian pick-up point in Toronto

CBC film news editor
in Toronto

News film editor at CBC station, Windsor, Ontario

The audience in Windsor, Ontario

ferent parts of that information, and in preparing that information for a newspaper or a broadcast, are likely to treat the information differently. Thus, in understanding gatekeeping processes, it should be kept in mind that there are both quantitative and qualitative considerations concerning information handling. When one looks at a specific event (such as outlined in Figure 2-4), and considers the many gates through which the report of that event passes, a question should quite legitimately be raised: in terms of accuracy, what is the relationship of the story as seen on a local television station in Windsor, Ontario to the event that occurred in Windsor, England?

The gatekeeper concept that Schramm developed for news flows had been used earlier (in 1943) by sociologist Kurt Lewin. Lewin coined the term "gatekeeper" as he studied food-selection habits: he described this activity as a cultural process whereby food comes to the table through various channels (buying, gardening, preparing, etc.).[24]

Research relating to the gatekeeper theory has thus far emphasized particular agents — people in decision-making positions — with regard to news content. A major study in this vein is David Manning White's analysis of news flows. White adapted Lewin's theory of the gatekeeper and applied it to the movement of a news story. He indicates, as does Schramm, how a sequence of individuals engage in selecting and discarding information.[25]

Gatekeeping is not purely a function based on individual behavior. Lewin states that gates are controlled "either by impartial rules or by 'gatekeepers.'"[26] If "impartial rules" may act as the control agent, it seems logical to suggest that there may be other such agents — organizations, for example — and that it may be useful to define gatekeeping in a broad, macro sense, rather than the narrower, micro manner in which it has been interpreted in the journalism literature. Following from this view, we offer the following definition: a gatekeeper is any social instititution, social context, activity or thing that has, as a consequence of its characteristics or behavior, the effect of modifying media content. Information movement and gatekeeping forces are diagrammed in Figure 2-5.

All media and media organizations work within the context of a culture which forms their operational environment, as Figure 2-5 indicates. Culture, organization, and media type can be seen as factors which influence the production of media content. In other words, the cultural environment, type of medium, and organizational context are *macro-gatekeepers*, while individuals performing various activities within these environments are the *micro-gatekeepers*.

Media output, we assume, must have some effect on, and elicit some response from, listeners and viewers. To some degree, this has already been discussed in preceding material. The idea of agenda-setting, however, appears to be the most useful theory for explaining the relationship between the media and the public. According to Donald L. Shaw and Maxwell E. McCombs,

> This impact of the mass media — the ability to effect cognitive change among individuals, to structure their thinking — has been labeled the

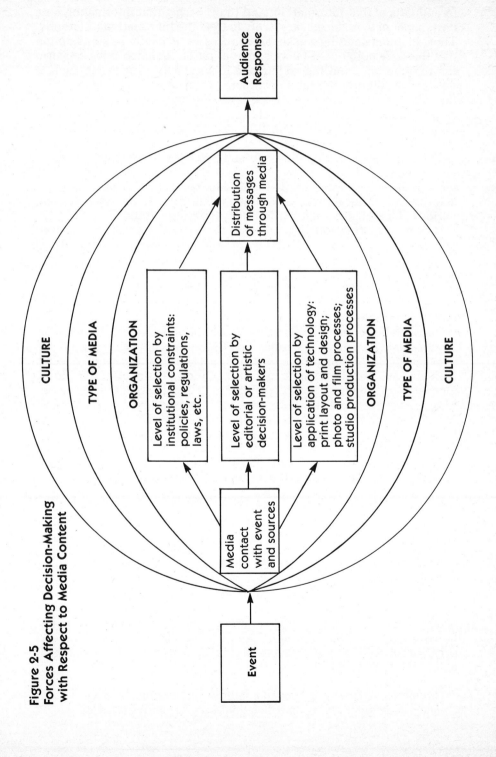

Figure 2-5
Forces Affecting Decision-Making
with Respect to Media Content

Audience Response

Distribution of messages through media

CULTURE

TYPE OF MEDIA

ORGANIZATION

Level of selection by institutional constraints: policies, regulations, laws, etc.

Level of selection by editorial or artistic decision-makers

Level of selection by application of technology: print layout and design; photo and film processes; studio production processes

ORGANIZATION

TYPE OF MEDIA

CULTURE

Media contact with event and sources

Event

agenda-setting function of mass communication. Here may lie the most important effect of mass communication, its ability to mentally order and organize our world for us.[27]

While some research has shown a weaker relationship between media and public agendas than that suggested by Shaw and McCombs, if their argument is accepted, it makes sense to examine radio and television news content, especially for the themes selected for prominence in the course of an event like an election. Where two elections are held in rapid succession, as was the case in Canada in 1979 and 1980, the researcher is afforded a rare opportunity to examine differences in political agendas as well as the news treatment of parties and party leaders by the media. Before embarking on such an exploration, however, a brief review of the American and Canadian literature relating media and elections is necessary.

Media and Elections: An Overview of the American Literature

As everyone is aware, elections which once could be said to be fought "on the hustings," from railway car platforms, and at mass rallies, must now be termed primarily media events. This was recognized earlier in the United States than elsewhere—probably because it first became true there. American scholars consequently also pioneered the systematic study of elections, and both because they originated some of the basic principles which have come to be accepted regarding media behavior during elections, and because their studies became the models for later Canadian studies, a review of the US literature is desirable here.

Perhaps the most intriguing aspect of the American literature on media and political campaigns is that, despite the assumed influence of media (as evidenced by the many millions of dollars that continue to be invested in media campaigns), attempts to establish a direct cause and effect relationship between media messages and voter attitudes or behavior have been inconclusive.

Nevertheless, it is clear that a relationship does exist between media messages and the electorate, and one can look to processes of persuasion to shed light on that relationship. Studies of propaganda, particularly those that followed World Wars I and II and the Korean War, indicate that:

- media messages can persuade, particularly by reinforcing existing opinions
- information from a new perspective with respect to existing opinions can bring about opinion change
- if receivers have weak or no opinions about particular matters, media information systems may well fill the void
- propagandists concede that if receivers of information have well-embedded opinions and attitudes, mass media information by itself is not likely to bring about change.[28]

While current research supports such thinking, the literature also reveals beliefs held by politicians and parties about effects on the electorate from mass media exposure which are not as well supported. It was felt, for example, that because mass media are inherently credible, the information that the media transmitted would persuade the electorate. While there is some doubt about such an effect, political parties have always been attracted to mass media, if for no other reason than that media reach voters in large numbers. We can go back to the early days of radio to trace the attraction that mass media have held for politicians.

As early as 1924, a desire to reach a large number of voters led to the development of radio networking, using a combination of telephone systems and shortwave broadcasting. In that year, the American presidential campaign between Calvin Coolidge and John W. Davis was characterized by extensive use of radio. On the eve of the election, for example, when Coolidge broadcast over 26 linked radio stations, it is estimated that his audience numbered twenty to thirty million listeners.[29]

From that election onward, radio broadcasting became a part of each political campaign, whether local, state, or national in scope. It also became clear in those early days that campaigning had changed drastically. While travelling by train from town to town to touch hands with the electorate continued for many years to be a popular electioneering format, it was clear that electronic transmissions touched many more listeners in one or two broadcasts than could be reached personally in a traditional presidential campaign.

Empirical, verifiable studies of political campaigns, based on survey research techniques, began in the United States in the early 1940s, and have added immeasurably to our knowledge about the link the media provide between the politician and the voter. The earliest of these was the 1940 presidential campaign, studied in Erie County, Ohio, by Paul Lazarsfeld and his colleagues.[30] In the process of studying the electorate to determine the effectiveness of various media in influencing the vote, it was with some surprise that the Lazarsfeld team discovered that interpersonal contacts were more influential in determining attitudes than were radio and the print media. It was out of such findings, reinforced by further research in 1948,[31] that the two-step flow of communication[32] and later multiple-step flow theories developed.

In the "two-step" pattern of information diffusion, information from the media is disseminated indirectly to the electorate through opinion-leaders, that is, people who are attentive to the media and who relay the information thus gained to their friends, workmates and families. Such an information flow pattern has come under challenge from two directions.

First, subsequent studies have indicated that news of a "shocking" nature is likely to be disseminated by word of mouth, but that the bulk of news in our society comes directly from the mass media. (In the future, the multiplication of media channels will increasingly segment audiences, so that the traditional two-step flow theory will take on less and less significance in information movement studies). Second, studies subsequent to the Lazarsfeld research indicate that opinion-leaders themselves have other opinion-leaders, thus suggesting a multi-step flow of information.[33] Nevertheless, it is due directly to the effort of Lazarsfeld and his colleagues that such revealing research into information, the media, and the electorate has been generated.

The Lazarsfeld studies utilized the panel approach, where a relatively small geographical area was sampled and respondents were interviewed at different periods in the course of the campaign. Beginning with the 1948 presidential election, Angus Campbell and a research team connected with the Institute for Social Research (ISR) at the University of Michigan began their studies of the American electorate. In the 1952 election, they utilized a national sample of voters. This election, along with data collected from another national sample in 1956, formed the basis for their seminal contribution to the study of voting behavior, *The American Voter*, published in 1960.[34]

Despite its pre-eminent reputation, the question of the role of media influencing electoral behavior was not actively pursued in *The American Voter*. The key variable advanced by the Campbell team to explain voting was party identification; mass media, given their prominence in the earlier Lazarsfeld studies, were curiously absent from the discussion.

This media gap was filled admirably by V. O. Key, who used the ISR data bank in researching his brilliant volume, *Public Opinion and American Democracy*. Key reviews the impact of mass media, mass media usage, media attentiveness and a host of other variables, such as political participation, level of education, and knowledge of campaign information. Key concluded that

> The flow of messages of the mass media is rather like dropping a handful of confetti from the rim of the Grand Canyon with the object of striking a man astride a burro on the canyon floor. In some measure chance determines which messages reach what targets.[35]

Key reintroduces the two-step and multi-step flow of communication models, pointing out the impact of interpersonal communication and group membership as factors blunting the impact of media messages.

In *Elections and the Political Order*,[36] the follow-up volume to *The American Voter*, mass media are again not especially high on the ISR research team's priorities. However, in one chapter, "Information Flow and the Stability of Partisan Attitudes," Philip Converse attempts to test the hypothesis that it is "the less involved and less informed voters" who are most likely to change their party affiliation.

In a closely reasoned analysis, Converse sees the electorate as relatively stable (a reflection of the strength and persistence of party identification as an anchoring device), but that short-term forces in any given electoral contest may work to weaken this basically stable condition.[37] In controlling the flow of information in campaigns, the media play a potentially crucial role in amplifying forces working for change. The paradox which Converse points out, and which serves to explain why media effects on voting decisions are not stronger, is that those with the weakest party identification, and therefore most likely to be influenced by media, are precisely those who are least likely to come into contact with media accounts of the campaign.[38]

Another aspect of the media's impact on the voting decisions of the American electorate has been the television debates between Presidential candidates. The Kennedy-Nixon debates of 1960 and the Ford-Carter debates of 1976 are the most widely studied.[39] Conclusions about media effects of these special events, which entail extraordinarily high voter interest, fall into the major pattern of media effects in general:

- all media information input is conditioned by strong predispositons such as party identification, ideology, and opinions about particular candidates
- relative to these predispositions, media impact is weak, due to such factors as lack of voter interest and low attention levels
- what information is assimilated tends to confirm pre-existing attitudes
- voters simply do not devote very much mental energy to making complex political choices.[40]

Sears and Chaffee conclude that in spite of expectations to the contrary, the debates do fit within the limited media effects principle outlined above in the discussion of propaganda:

> Hence, despite the expanded exposure, debates would be expected mainly to reinforce both the standing party allegiances and the candidate preferences built up over the many prior months of campaigning, primary elections, and conventions. The genuinely uncommitted voter might, of course, well be influenced to choose sides by a superior performance by one candidate.[41]

Overall, empirical research on the impact of media on elections in the United States is at best inconclusive. However, as inconclusive as this research on media effects is, politicians and their advisors continue to devote the majority of their campaign strategy, and consequently their campaign budgets, attempting to reach the voter through the mass media.

Media and Elections: The Canadian Literature

Empirical studies on the role of media in Canadian elections are of more recent vintage and, while growing, they are not nearly as extensive as their American counterparts. This literature can therefore be reviewed in greater detail than was the case with the American studies.

In general, there are two broad categories of Canadian literature: (1) voting studies (where media are treated as one factor in influencing the voting decision) and (2) media studies, where the behavior of the media in a campaign is the major focus of study.

The Voting Literature

Serious study of elections in Canada began with the campaigns in 1957 and 1958. Sparked by the desire to understand the reasons for the ouster of the 22-year Liberal regime in 1957 and to explain the sheer magnitude of the Conservative victory (including their breakthrough in Quebec) in 1958, scholars like John Meisel, Peter Regenstrief, Harold Scarrow, and Denis Wrong began more detailed and comprehensive studies of the campaigns than had been previously attempted.[42] They were primarily interested in similarities and differences in campaign strategies, the age, occupation and other attributes of candidates, the role and impact of party leaders, and voting patterns across the country.

In the first book-length election study, *The Canadian General Election of 1957*, John Meisel complained that the greatest handicap in such work was "the dearth of attitude studies of the electorate based on adequate sample surveys."[43] For his *Papers on the 1962 Election*,[44] he tried to overcome this deficiency by asking 15 scholars representing various parts of Canada to contribute essays on those aspects of the election that happened to interest them. The results, though interesting and more comprehensive than the first book, were still not based on a single, consistent, nation-wide body of data, such as would have allowed the production of a Canadian counterpart to *The American Voter*. Funding for large sample survey work would not be made available until the election of 1965. This permitted a more scientifically sound and concentrated analysis of voters, and the effects of such factors as religion, age, sex, occupation, and social class on voting behavior. Meisel's third book, *Working Papers on Canadian Politics*,[45] based on a national sample, was admittedly preliminary, intended to publish data as quickly as possible. Noteworthy for our purposes was the absence of data regarding the impact of the media. Other highly regarded scholars in the field of voting studies of the late 1960s and early 1970s include Jean Laponce, Maurice Pinard, and Vincent Lemieux, who produced many widely read articles and monographs.

The late 1970s produced another generation of students of voting behavior, including David Elkins, Donald Blake, Harold Clarke, Jane Jensen, Lawrence LeDuc, and Jon Pammett. These last four produced, on the basis of a national election survey of the 1974 election, the most comprehensive study available on voter behavior in Canada, *Political Choice in Canada*.[46] This has been followed by other studies of the 1979 and 1980 elections.

For our purposes, what is extremely helpful is a chapter on the role of the media in influencing voter decisions. Indeed, media in Canadian elections appear to take on a particularly salient role, since that research group finds that beneath the apparent stability that might be deduced from an almost unbroken string of Liberal victories in the modern era, a great deal of flexible partisanship is induced by short-term factors that generate vote switching in all possible directions.[47]

The discussion of political campaigns by the authors of *Political Choice in Canada* focuses on newspaper treatment of the campaign and the use voters made of that material. With respect to media information, first of all it was "national" in scope and focused mainly on party leaders.[48] Their study shows as well that television emerges as the leading information medium, followed closely by newspapers and more distantly by radio. The impact of this media campaign information in Canada, as has been reported in the American literature, is not readily identifiable. Vote switchers from 1972 to 1974 were no more likely to have been heavy media users than were those whose vote remained stable.[49] Thus we remain gripped by the paradox of everyone believing that the media have great influence, and spending accordingly, while social scientists continue to search in vain for conclusive evidence that this is indeed the case.

The Media Literature

The media in Canada have been subjected to scholarly research for many decades, and we have reviewed the highlights of media development in Canada in Chapter 1. This interest has been augmented by a succession of Royal Commissions and committees (to be discussed in Chapter 5), which have investigated the role and regulation of the media. Systematic analysis of the content of the media has been a more contemporary phenomenon. Work on the content of the media in election periods has not been attempted until recent times.

The first systematic study of media content in Canadian election campaigns was T. H. Qualter's and K. A. MacKirdy's, "The Press of Ontario and the Election," in Meisel's *Papers on the 1962 Election.* Qualter and MacKirdy analyzed the election content of eight Ontario newspapers for items such as total space devoted to each party, assessment of each paper's partisanship as expressed in a ratio of favorable to unfavorable comments, and positioning of material in the paper. Major findings of this study include the range of the ratio of news space devoted to each party: 30.5% to 39.0% for the governing Conservatives, 18.1% to 29.3% for the Liberals, and 7.0% to 10.8% for the NDP.[50] From the Qualter and MacKirdy data, the predominant role of the press in the 1962 election appears to have been that of cheerleader for all of the major parties, as each paper displayed more positive than negative coverage of each of them.[51]

Other research on this subject includes the Wagenberg and Soderlund studies concerning the effects of chain-ownership on newspaper editorial content in the 1972[52] and 1974[53] elections. In both elections, editorialists, regardless of newspaper or chain, tended to indentify the same set of issues as critical to the campaign, and, perhaps more important, to evaluate all parties in the same (negative) way. The latter is in significant contrast to the Qualter-MacKirdy findings. Assuming the differences are not accounted for by differences in research methods in the two studies, it would appear that Canadian media changed from a generally positive portrayal of parties, their platforms, and their leaders to a much more critical perspective of all of them in the space of ten years.

The media role in the 1974 campaign was examined in a more comprehensive manner by Frederick J. Fletcher.[54] In addition to presenting a general overview of media organization and party media strategies,

Fletcher analyzed a sample of front, editorial, and special election pages
of sixteen Canadian newspapers. Fletcher concludes:

> Despite an unsympathetic press corps, the Liberals dominated the front
> pages of Canada's newspapers during the campaign.... The Liberals
> obtained more coverage than other parties in twelve of the sixteen dailies
> surveyed and were tied with the Conservatives in three others. The
> Conservatives led in only one paper and actually trailed the Liberals in
> four of the five papers which endorsed them.[55]

Fletcher also presented aggregate data on the amount of time that networks devoted to the major parties, both free time and news. In general,
these data confirm the Qualter-MacKirdy findings that the governing
party has the edge in media coverage.

The 1979 and 1980 elections were without doubt the most extensively
studied in Canadian history. In addition to the national election surveys
conducted by the Clarke, Jensen, LeDuc, Pammett group, the media role
was studied in a variety of other ways. Besides our own content analysis
studies, which will be described shortly, Fletcher and R. Jeremy Wilson
examined overall media coverage, William O. Gilsdorf conducted extensive interviews with both party and media officials regarding their respective strategies for waging and covering the campaign, while Clive
Cocking studied the performance of the press corps, through participant
observation.

Fletcher's evaluation of the media's impact on the 1979 and 1980 elections is found in a background paper that he prepared for a symposium,
"Politics and the Media," held in Toronto in June 1980. This paper formed
the basis for Fletcher's chapter, "Playing the Game: The Mass Media in
the 1979 Campaign," in Howard R. Penniman's edited work, *Canada
and the Polls, 1979-1980: A Study of the General Elections.*[56] Fletcher
presents the campaigns as essentially being "run for the news media."
He characterizes the process as "the contest waged by the parties and
their leaders to determine the issues around which the national (i.e.
media) campaign will revolve. The object of the contest ... is to manage
events so that the news coverage will come out as close to their preferred
version of events as possible."[57] Fletcher found campaign coverage
increasing in volume from 1974 to 1979, then falling off in 1980. He
concludes that, although they lost the 1979 election, the Liberals "won"
the 1979 media campaign, while in 1980, although the Conservatives
ran a high-pressure campaign, as opposed to a laid-back effort on the
part of the Liberals, media coverage was about equal. Fletcher also dis-
cusses the consequences of media-dominated elections for the general
health of democratic systems, which we shall address in our concluding
chapter.

R. Jeremy Wilson has criticized the media coverage of the 1979 and
1980 election campaigns. His analysis of selected newspapers and television news broadcasts revealed that the largest category of coverage could
be depicted as "horserace commentary": elections were reported as

contests, with strategies, polls, and campaign techniques being accorded wide attention. According to Wilson, this was done at the cost of in-depth analysis of issues. Television has contributed to this approach. On television the portrayal of ideas is more difficult than is the visual presentation of leaders, especially in conflict with other leaders. The parties, in reaction to the emphasis placed on this type of election reporting, engage in what Wilson calls a "meta-campaign." They attempt to show the public that they can wage a slick and efficient campaign, thus giving evidence of their winning style and their capacity to govern. Wilson feels this horserace approach de-emphasizes the educational value of elections and denies the electorate the basis upon which to analyze issues.[58]

William O. Gilsdorf's study of the 1979 and 1980 elections focused on the interaction of party strategists and network officials and is based on extensive in-depth interviews. Gilsdorf concludes that "most party resources were put into a leader tour and most press strategies went into a national media focus."[59] This, according to Gilsdorf, accentuated leader-ship as the dominant issue in the campaigns. His research shows how the Liberal Party manipulated the leadership dimension, by either high-lighting the positive attributes of Mr. Trudeau in 1979, or attempting to exploit the weaknesses of Mr. Clark in 1980. In both instances, Gilsdorf sees a convergence "between what the Liberals preferred to have as the election agenda and what the media perceived as the important issues."[60]

For Clive Cocking, the working press was the subject of investigation. In a strategy reminiscent of that used by Timothy Crouse to study the reporting to the American presidential campaign in 1972,[61] Cocking presents, in an edited diary form, his observations of the press and the campaign. As stated by Cocking: "I had gone out to observe the news media in their natural habitat, much like an anthropologist studying some strange lost nomadic tribe."[62] While the book is largely anecdotal, Cock-ing does document the way in which the three major parties catered to the press. His general conclusion is that the campaign was run primar-ily for television. In addition, we are given a glimpse of the media peck-ing order and an appreciation for the workings of pack journalism.

While the Canadian literature on the mass media and elections is not as extensive as the American literature, it is reassuring to see that the Canadian researchers are beginning to fill a void that was quite apparent only a few years ago. The empirical data that form the basis for Chapters 3 and 4, and which will be described in the following paragraphs, is our effort to advance the study of the relationship between media and elec-tions in Canada. Specifically, we wanted to study the message portion of the communication act. Our goal is to document, in as much detail as possible, the campaign information transmitted to Canadian voters in 1979 and 1980 by French and English television and radio, and in the earlier year, by newspapers in all regions of the country. Since such an examination had never been done, it appeared to be a logical next step in advancing knowledge in this area.

The Research Design

The data presented in the following two chapters, dealing with electronic media and print media coverage of the 1979 and 1980 campaigns, are based on content analysis methods. Chapter 3 contains analysis of the electronic media. Four major television networks and two radio networks were selected for study: CBC French television, CBC English television, Global television, and the Canadian Television Network (CTV); Radio Canada (the French-language radio network), and the CBC English radio network.

Video and audio recordings of the major evening newscast of each day were made for each network. These tapes were systematically analyzed for thematic content, evaluative material on political parties and party leaders, as well as for such variables as placement in the broadcast and time devoted to each story. Since stories were rarely unidimensional, each news theme appearing in a given story was coded.

Some differences between the 1979 and 1980 data sets used in Chapter 3 need to be clarified. First, the 1979 election was long awaited and predictable as to the approximate time it would be called. Therefore, we were prepared in advance and began recording on the day the election was called, and continued on a daily basis throughout the campaign. In 1980, however, the situation was quite different. We were as surprised as Mr. Clark when his government fell, and consequently during the first four weeks of the campaign, due to uncertainties in funding, we were able to record newscasts only on every third day. However, for the final four weeks of the campaign, we returned to the daily recording of newscasts.

Although this results in a 1980 data set containing fewer stories than that for 1979, we are nonetheless satisfied that this does not seriously damage their comparability. In part this is so since the early stages of the 1980 campaign coincided with the Christmas–New Year holiday period, during which little campaigning was done. In any case, the 1979 electronic data set contains 1,758 stories as compared to 1,227 for 1980. In both election periods approximately one-third of all new stories broadcast in our sample were election oriented: 31.9% in 1979 and 33.8% in 1980.

Chapter 4 presents data on print coverage of the 1979 campaign. We examined twenty-three newspapers, representing every province and both official languages. As with the electronic media, in the 1979 campaign, all of these newspapers were examined daily for the duration of the campaign. We did not, however, analyze all of the election content in the papers. Rather we examined all front page stories, editorials, editorial-page and opposite-editorial-page features, and editorial cartoons. Thematic content and evaluative commentary on political parties and party leaders were coded. The resulting newspaper data set for 1979 contains 5,187 items: 1,876 front page stories, 1,045 editorials, 1,576 features, and 570 cartoons.[63]

Our data do not represent the total campaign dialogue, nor do they reveal what particular parties or Canadians, in general, were thinking during the campaigns. The data do represent what leading television and radio networks and major newspapers throughout Canada selected from the entire day's campaign activity for presentation to the Canadian public in capsule form in their major daily newscasts, or in the case of newspapers, reported on their front pages, or commented on in editorials, features, and cartoons. Stated differently, we studied the political information that passed through the various gates and constituted the media agenda for the 1979 and 1980 Canadian elections.

Notes

[1]UNESCO, *Many Voices, One World: Report of the International Commission for the Study of Communication Problems* (New York: Unipub, 1980), p. 58.

[2]Ibid.

[3]"Study Finds Massive Illiteracy in the U.S.," Toronto *Globe and Mail*, September 11, 1979, p. 14.

[4]UNESCO, *Statistical Reports and Studies: Statistics of Educational Attainment and Literacy, 1945-1974* (Paris: The UNESCO Press, 1977), p. 12.

[5]UNESCO, *The Experimental World Literacy Programme: A Critical Assessment* (Paris: The UNESCO Press, 1976).

[6]Amadou-Mahtar M'Bow, *UNESCO and the Solidarity of Nations: Building the Future* (Paris: The UNESCO Press, 1980), p. 158.

[7]UNESCO, *Many Voices, One World*, p. 53.

[8]See Alan Booth, "The Recall of News Items," *Public Opinion Quarterly*, 34 (1970-71), pp. 604-10; Nikos Metallinos and Robert K. Tiemens, "Assumptions of the Screen: The Effect of Left Versus Right Placement of Television Images," *Journal of Broadcasting*, 21 (Winter 1977), pp. 21-33; and Thomas A. McCain, Joseph Chilberg, and Jacob Wakshlag, "The Effect of Camera Angle on Source Creditability and Attraction," *Journal of Broadcasting*, 21 (Winter 1977), pp. 35-46.

[9]A detailed discussion of the rewards of television programming and the rewards of formal curricular training, as well as discussion of other comparisons of TV and the school are contained in Neil Postman, "The First Curriculum: Comparing School and Television," *Phi Delta Kappan*, 60 (November 1979), pp. 163-168.

[10]See UNESCO, *Many Voices, One World*, p. 228. The UNESCO Commission cites data collected and compiled by Marc V. Porat, "Communication Policy in an Information Society," in Glen O. Robinson, ed., *Communications for Tomorrow: Policy Perspectives in the 1980's* (Toronto: Praeger Publishers, 1978), pp. 3-60.

[11]UNESCO, *Many Voices, One World*, p. 270.

[12]"A larger group of persons linked by...complementary habits and facilities of communication we may call a people." See Karl W. Deutsch, *Nationalism and Social Communication: An Inquiry into the Foundations of Nationality* (Cambridge: Massachusetts Institute of Technology, 1966), p. 96.

[13]Lester Thonssen, A. Craig Baird, and Waldo W. Braden, *Speech Criticism* (New York: Ronald Press, 1970), p. 33.

[14]Ibid., p. 63.

[15]Harold D. Lasswell, "The Structure and Function of Communication in Society," in L. Bryson, ed., *The Communication of Ideas* (New York: Harper and Brothers, 1948), pp. 37-51.

[16]In fact, the "more just and more efficient world information order" became the working title of the UNESCO Commission. To modify such developing concentration of information sources and new technologies, the Commission recommended that "national and international measures are required, among them reform of existing patent laws and conventions, appropriate legislation and international agreements." See UNESCO, *Many Voices, One World*, p. 259.

[17]For example, see Morris Janowitz and Paul Hirsch, eds., *Reader in Public Opinion and Mass Communication*, 3rd ed. (New York: Free Press, 1981).

[18]Joseph T. Klapper, *The Effects of Mass Communication* (New York: Free Press, 1960), p. 22.

[19]Ibid., p. 19.

[20]Ibid.

[21]Jay G. Blumler, "The Role of Theory in Uses and Gratifications Studies," *Communication Research*, 6 (January 1979), pp. 9-36.

[22]Elihu Katz, "The Uses of Becker, Blumler, and Swanson," *Communication Research*, 6 (January 1979), p. 74-83.

[23]Wilber Schramm, "The Gatekeeper: A Memorandum," in Wilbur Schramm, ed., *Mass Communications* (Urbana: University of Illinois Press, 1972), p. 175.

[24]Kurt Lewin, "Psychological Ecology," in Dorwin Cartwright, ed., *Field Theory in Social Sciences* (New York: Harper and Bros., 1951), pp. 174-177.

[25]David Manning White, "The Gatekeeper: A Study in the Selection of News," *Journalism Quarterly*, 27 (Fall 1950), p. 384.

[26]Lewin, p. 186 (emphasis is ours). Extending the definition of "gatekeeping," guided by Lewin's reference to "impartial rules," was started in 1973 in an attempt to develop a perspective from which a critic of mass media might evaluate media content. See Walter I. Romanow, "The Study of Gatekeepers in Mass Media: A Stance for the Mass Media Critic," Unpublished paper, University of Windsor, Ontario, 1973.

[27]Donald L. Shaw and Maxwell E. McCombs, *The Emergence of American Political Issues: The Agenda-Setting Function of the Press* (St. Paul, Minnesota: West Publishing, 1977), p. 5 (emphasis is in the original). An excellent summary of theories and researches associated with agenda-setting, as well as comprehensive bibliography, are contained in this book.

[28]Thus totalitarian governments such as the Nazi, Fascist, and Communist regimes in the twentieth century attempted to eradicate or neutralize the social forces that create divergent and strongly held opinions in a society and therefore cut off the roots of the well-embedded traditions that provided the foundations for such strong beliefs.

[29]Lewis E. Weeks, "The Radio Election of 1924," *Journal of Broadcasting*, 8 (Summer 1964), p. 233-243.

[30]Bernard R. Berelson, Paul F. Lazarsfeld, and Hazel Gaudet, *The People's Choice* (New York: Columbia University Press, 1944).

[31]Bernard R. Berelson, Paul F. Lazarsfeld, and William N. McPhee, *Voting* (Chicago: University of Chicago Press, 1954).

[32]Elihu Katz and Paul F. Lazarsfeld, *Personal Influence: The Part Played by People in the Flow of Mass Communications* (New York: Free Press, 1955).

[33]See Wilbur Schramm and William E. Porter, *Men, Women, Messages, and Media* (New York: Harper and Row, 1982), pp. 110-114, where the studies of information diffusion are discussed. See also B. S. Greenberg, "Person-to-Person Communication in the Diffusion of News Events," *Journalism Quarterly*, 41 (1964); and V. C. Trohldahl, "A Field Test of a Modified 'Two-Step Flow of Communication' Model," *Public Opinion Quarterly*, 30 (1966-1967), pp. 609-623.

[34]Angus Campbell, Philip Converse, Warren E. Miller, and Donald E. Stokes, *The American Voter* (New York: John Wiley and Sons, 1960).

[35]V. O. Key Jr., *Public Opinion and American Democracy* (New York: Alfred A. Knopf, 1967).

[36]Angus Campbell, Philip E. Converse, Warren E. Miller, and Donald E. Stokes, *Elections and the Political Order* (New York: John Wiley and Sons, 1966).

[37]Philip E. Converse, "Information Flow and the Stability of Partisan Attitudes," in *Elections and the Political Order*, pp. 140-141.

[38]Ibid., pp. 143-147.

[39]For the best overall accounts, see Sidney Kraus, ed., *The Great Debates: Background, Perspectives, Effects* (Bloomington: Indiana University Press, 1962) and Sidney Kraus, ed., *The Great Debates: Carter vs. Ford, 1976* (Bloomington: Indiana University Press, 1979).

[40]David O. Sears and Steven H. Chaffee, "Uses and Effects of the 1976 Debates: An Overview of Empirical Studies," in *The Great Debates: Carter vs. Ford*, p. 227.

[41]Ibid., p. 253.

[42]See, for instance, John Meisel, *The Canadian Election of 1957* (Toronto: University of Toronto Press, 1962); John Meisel "Formulation of Liberal and Conservative Programs in the 1957 Canadian General Election," *Canadian Journal of Economics and Political Science*, 26 (1960); Peter Regenstrief, "The Canadian General Election of 1958," *Western Political Quarterly*, 13 (1960); Harold Scarrow, "Federal-Provincial Voting Patterns in Canada," *Canadian Journal of Economics and Political Science*, 26 (1960); Harold Scarrow "Patterns of Voter Turnout in Canada," *Midwest Journal of Political Science*, 5 (1961); and Denis H. Wrong, "The Pattern of Party Voting in Canada," *Public Opinion Quarterly*, 21 (1957).

[43]Meisel, *The General Election of 1957*, preface, p. VIII.

[44]John Meisel, ed., *Papers on the 1962 Election* (Toronto: University of Toronto Press, 1964).

[45]John Meisel, *Working Papers on Canadian Politics*, 2nd Enlarged Ed. (Montreal: McGill-Queen's University Press, 1975).

[46]Harold D. Clarke, Jane Jensen, Lawrence LeDuc, and Jon Pammett, *Political Choice in Canada* (Toronto: McGraw-Hill Ryerson, 1979).

[47]Ibid., see Chapter 10.

[48]Ibid., p. 279.

[49]Ibid., p. 290.

[50]T. H. Qualter and K. A. MacKirdy, "The Press of Ontario and the Election," in *Papers on the 1962 Election*, p. 147.

[51]Ibid., pp. 150-151.

[52]Ronald H. Wagenberg and Walter C. Soderlund, ''The Influence of Chain-Ownership on Editorial Comment in Canada,'' *Journalism Quarterly*, 52 (Spring 1975), pp. 93-98.

[53]Ronald H. Wagenberg and Walter C. Soderlund, ''The Effects of Chain Ownership on Editorial Coverage: The Case of the 1974 Canadian Federal Election,'' *Canadian Journal of Political Science*, IX (December 1976), pp. 683-689.

[54]Frederick J. Fletcher, ''The Mass Media in the 1974 Canadian Election,'' in Howard R. Penniman, ed., *Canada at the Polls: The General Election of 1974* (Washington: American Enterprise Institute for Public Policy Research, 1975).

[55]Ibid., p. 265.

[56]Frederick J. Fletcher, ''The Contest for Media Attention: The 1979 and 1980 Federal Election Campaigns,'' in *Politics and the Media: An examination of the issues raised by the Quebec Referendum and the 1979 and 1980 Federal Elections* (Toronto: The Reader's Digest Foundation of Canada, 1981); and ''Playing the Game: The Mass Media and the 1979 Campaign,'' in Howard R. Penniman, ed., *Canada at the Polls, 1979 and 1980: A Study of the General Elections* (Washington: American Enterprise Institute For Public Policy Research, 1981).

[57]Fletcher, ''The Contest for Media Attention,'' pp. 125-126.

[58]R. Jeremy Wilson, ''Media Coverage of Canadian Election Campaigns: Horserace Journalism and the Meta-Campaign,'' *Journal of Canadian Studies*, 15 (Winter 1980-1981), pp. 56-68.

[59]William O. Gilsdorf, ''Getting the Message Across: The Communication Strategy of the Federal Liberal Party in the 1979 and 1980 Canadian Federal Elections.'' Paper presented to the Annual Meeting of the Canadian Communication Association, Université du Québec à Montréal, 1980, p. 43. This paper is reprinted in an abridged form, ''Getting the Message Across: Media Strategies and Political Campaigns,'' in Liora Salter, ed., *Communication Studies in Canada* (Toronto: Butterworth's, 1981), pp. 52-67.

[60]Ibid., p. 5.

[61]Timothy Crouse, *The Boys on the Bus* (New York: Ballantine Books, 1972).

[62]Clive Cocking, *Following the Leaders: A Media Watcher's Diary of Campaign '79* (Toronto: Doubleday Canada Ltd., 1980), p. 2.

[63]Intercoder Reliability for the 1979 data was established at 83.7% using the formula $CR = \dfrac{2M}{N_1 + N_2}$, while that for the 1980 data was 87.7%. See Ole Holsti, *Content Analysis for the Social Sciences and Humanities* (Reading, Mass.: Addison-Wesley, 1969), p. 40.

3

Television and Radio
Reporting of the 1979
and 1980 Campaigns

The elections of 1979 and 1980 presented Canadian researchers with a major opportunity to study the electronic media in the context of the theories discussed in Chapter 2. Gatekeeping and agenda-setting have particularly interested us, and the two elections taking place so close to each other provide a unique opportunity for comparative analysis. By 1979 the pre-eminent role of television in the campaign strategies of the parties had been established. The dictates of that medium guided the parties' attempts to establish the issues and themes that they hoped would dominate the public's perception of the election. Radio played a lesser but not inconsequential part in election coverage. Beyond that an analysis of radio coverage allowed us a comparison of the two electronic media for differences in their treatment of campaign material.

This chapter gives an account of how the electronic media (radio and television, as well as different networks both public and private) reported on the issues, leaders, and parties that provided the substance of the election. Before embarking on that portrayal, however, it will be helpful to review briefly the context in which the two elections took place.

Background to the Elections

The unusually long interval between the 1974 election and the successive ones of 1979 and 1980 ensured that the latter two would take place in substantially different circumstances than the first. By ignoring custom and allowing the five-year life of Parliament nearly to expire before calling an election, Prime Minister Trudeau entered the 1979 election facing an altered electorate, an increased number of seats to be contested, new leadership in all three opposition parties, and a new set of issues to be resolved.

Fully 15% of the 1979 electorate were new voters. While some of these were immigrants who had recently become citizens, the majority were those who had reached voting age (18) since 1974.[1] Any trend by these new voters toward one party could affect the results in many constituencies and perhaps even determine who would govern.

There were eighteen new seats available in 1979 and 1980, and the boundaries of almost all constituencies had been altered on the basis of the redistribution (not yet accomplished in 1974) occasioned by the 1971 census. The western provinces, especially BC and Alberta, were the biggest winners in increased representation, with nine new seats, bringing their total to 77. For the first time since the 1940s, the west had more seats than Quebec, which had an increase of one seat to a total of 75.

Since the west was the basis of Progressive Conservative strength, and also lent some support to the NDP, while the Liberals looked to Quebec for electoral support, these changes were of considerable significance. The key to the election, however, was populous Ontario, where the number of seats had risen from 88 to 95.[2]

The cast of characters in the election drama, aside from Liberal leader Pierre Trudeau, had changed almost completely since 1974. Robert Stanfield, having lost three successive campaigns, resigned the Progressive Conservative leadership in 1976. On the fourth ballot of the subsequent leadership convention, a little-known "dark horse" MP from Alberta named Joe Clark, whose obscurity led the media to dub him Joe Who, emerged victorious. He inherited a party long beset with internal discord. By the time of the 1979 election he appeared to have unified his party, though his personal image problem had not been entirely overcome.

In the NDP, David Lewis, who had suffered personal defeat in his constituency in 1974, yielded to Ed Broadbent, a leading member of the parliamentary caucus. The Social Credit Party (or Raillement Créditiste in Quebec, where it held its only seats) had lost its flamboyant populist leader, Real Caouette. After a succession of leaders, he was ultimately replaced by Fabien Roy in the first week of the 1979 election. What impact these new leaders might make on the electorate, and indeed what kind of "media image" they would be given in their first campaign, was subject to speculation.

While Trudeau still led the Liberals, the upper echelons of that party had lost John Turner and Donald MacDonald, both possible successors. This development lent credence to the complaint of many English-speaking Canadians that Trudeau led a francophone-dominated party.

Events since 1974 had accentuated the importance of a number of issues. National unity has been a persistent problem in Canadian politics, and the election of René Lévesque at the head of a Parti Québecois provincial government in 1976 created a new sense of urgency in Quebec's relations with the rest of Canada. Although Lévesque campaigned on the basis of providing a competent and honest alternative to the Bourassa government and downplayed his separatist policy, he lost no opportunity once in office to foster the cause of a politically independent Quebec, though one that would maintain an economic association with Canada. Language legislation was a priority, with the objective being an officially and functionally unilingual French-speaking province. The legislation provisions affected education, business, and social life and accordingly created disquiet among English-speaking Quebeckers and outright hostility outside the province's borders. Not the least of the effects of this policy was the movement of anglophone-dominated companies out of the province.

Other provinces, especially Alberta, were also becoming restive with what they perceived to be unwarranted federal intervention in provincial areas of concern. This was especially the case with regard to the control of resources, particularly oil and natural gas, the importance of which was magnified by a world-wide oil crisis. The conflict between oil-producing and oil-consuming countries was internalized in Canada because of Alberta's role as an oil producer. The federal government's resistance to world prices for Alberta oil created strains on the federal system because it denied Alberta (and some other provinces to a more limited extent) the full potential benefits of its scarce resource. Eastern Canada was the beneficiary of federal oil policy, and in addition, all Canadians had to shoulder the cost of the subsidy to bring the cost of imported oil down. The resultant budget drain created financial problems for the federal government, which became all the more intent on getting as large a share of the tax revenues from oil and natural gas as possible. Alberta's outrage was not hard to understand.

The problems engendered by Quebec specifically, and federal-provincial relations generally, fostered a resolve by the Trudeau government to bring about constitutional reform. A Task Force on National Unity was appointed in July 1977 and draft legislation to alter the constitution was introduced in June 1978. The thrust of the federal initiative was to patriate the constitution, establish an amending formula, entrench civil and linguistic rights, and restructure federal institutions, such as the Senate and the Supreme Court, to ensure regional input at the national level. However, the provinces' chief interest, the redistribution of legislative powers, was not addressed, and Mr. Trudeau in fact continued to emphasize the need for a strong central government and to attack those who would undermine its strength. Mr. Clark responded that Mr. Trudeau was too strident and that he, the Progressive Conservative leader, would be more conciliatory and better able to deal with the provincial premiers. There were no Liberal premiers by the date of the 1979 election, their last premier having been defeated in Prince Edward Island earlier that year.

The government was accused of using a constitutional smokescreen to distract attention from a serious economic situation. The Quebec situation and the oil crisis were factors that had contributed to the declining value of the Canadian dollar and budget deficits of worrisome magnitude. Inflation and high interest rates were accompanied by slow economic growth — so-called stagflation. Government spending was branded by conservative economists and businessmen as a major cause of inflation and high interest rates. The role and size of government became a subject of intense political debate. Wage and price controls, which had been ridiculed when proposed by Stanfield in 1974, were adopted by the Trudeau government in 1975. The brake they put on inflation was only temporary and the problem worsened to the accompaniment of higher rates of unemployment. The state of the economy, therefore, was a vital issue in 1979 and 1980, and PC proposals to relieve the impact of mortgage interest and property taxes found considerable public support. Generally, the state of the Canadian economy in 1979 was not good for a government seeking re-election; hence the delay in calling the election.

This brief review of changes in the Canadian political environment between 1974 and the 1979 and 1980 elections touches only the most significant issues. It does, however, indicate that a somewhat altered electorate would be choosing an enlarged and redistributed House of Commons, and, with the exception of Trudeau, would be assessing new party leaders. The voters would be doing so in a context of an intensified national unity crisis, which had spawned a variety of proposals for constitutional change. Moreover, economic uncertainty and dislocation were at their worst level in the post-war era. Five years had seen major changes in the Canadian political landscape.

The 1979 and 1980 Agenda

The environment within which media operate during electoral campaigns is more structured than would be the case in normal times, since the political parties attempt to mold the context of election into a form suitable for their own fortunes. To have to react to unforeseen and potentially uncontrollable events during the relatively brief campaign is the ultimate nightmare for party strategists. This is not to say that political parties do not continuously try to direct political commentary in a self-serving manner, but rather that this desire becomes extreme, indeed all-consuming, during election campaigns. In this sense the 1979 and 1980 elections were no exception, as William Gilsdorf has observed.[3] The media are aware of these attempts to manipulate them, but the structural dictates of the media and precepts of journalistic fair play conspire to allow shrewd political operators to deliver the message they want through the media. The politicians' hands are strengthened because they control access by granting or withholding interviews with the press. Thus despite the resentment many members of the media felt about Liberal conduct in the 1974 campaign (where Trudeau had blatantly timed releases of complicated campaign announcements, often lengthy ones, to provide little time for analysis[4]) their reporting of the campaigns that occupy our interest now was not dramatically different.

In this respect, R. Jeremy Wilson has commented upon the lack of issue-oriented analysis in the 1979-1980 campaigns.[5] Can the political parties be held wholly responsible for this? The media give no indication that, left to their own devices, they would do anything dramatically different than report on the leaders' national tours and the relatively few issues that parties stress during elections. For example, there is not much to prevent the media from providing in-depth reporting of the foreign policy stances of the various parties, but they seem reluctant to take this initiative, even when serious international events would seem to dictate media interest.[6]

In line with our view that a wide variety of social, technological, and organizational processes (as well as individuals) contribute to the gatekeeping and agenda-setting functions, we have examined the reporting of the 1979 and 1980 election campaigns by the electronic media in an attempt to discover the contributions of three macro-gates. The first of these is the organizational one, operationalized by the television or radio network transmitting the news. The second gate, following directly from our extended definition of gatekeeping, is the medium (radio or television) through which the news was transmitted. The third gate is a cultural one, operationalized by the language of broadcast, and prompted by the hypothesis that in Canada French and English media systems project different agendas to their listening and viewing publics.[7]

Issue Coverage by Frequency of Mention

Our findings on campaign issues, as shown in Tables 3-1 and 3-2, confirm the widely held view that leadership (including leaders' actions, personalities, and perceived competence) was the most important issue overall in both campaigns, but more dramatically in 1980. This finding is consistent with Gilsdorf's interview data, which show that the Liberals and Conservatives in the two elections desired to stress leadership, as did the NDP in 1980.[8] The NDP, traditionally an intensely issue-oriented party, had begun to lay greater stress on leadership as early as 1974, in an attempt to capitalize on the dynamic qualities of David Lewis.

All media outlets except Radio Canada carried a substantially greater proportion of leadership-oriented stories in 1980 than in 1979. There are various reasons for this intensified interest in leadership in 1980. The Liberals' withering attack on the competence of Joe Clark produced many stories, while the Conservatives were reminding the voters that they would have to suffer the leadership of Pierre Trudeau once again should the Liberals regain office. The New Democrats reacted to polls that showed that their leader, Ed Broadbent, outstripped the party in popularity, and stressed their leader more than had been the case previously.

Beyond the issue of leadership the media agenda in 1979 and 1980 show considerable variation. In 1979 the Liberal Party, at the insistence of Mr. Trudeau, sought to make national unity a major campaign issue.[9] The amount of coverge that was accorded this theme reflects the success of Liberal efforts. Many voters, especially in Quebec, shared Trudeau's assessment of the importance of the national unity issue. But as Harold Clarke and his colleagues point out, other issues that were more prominent in public opinion were less advantageous to the Liberals.[10] In the 1980 campaign, even though the Quebec referendum was scheduled for May in that year, national unity dropped from the top ten election issues.

Table 3-1 — Percentage of Electoral Stories Dealing with Major Issues in the 1979 Campaign by TV and Radio Networks (with Rank Order)

NETWORK

CAMPAIGN ISSUE	(Television)								(Radio)			
	CBC/FR (N=322) %	R/O	CBC/ENG (N=306) %	R/O	GLOBAL (N=345) %	R/O	CTV (N=259) %	R/O	RADIO CANADA (N=266) %	R/O	CBC RADIO (N=260) %	R/O
Leadership	26.7	(1)	23.2	(2)	21.7	(1)	28.2	(1)	18.0	(1)	14.2	(2)
National Unity	22.4	(2)	24.2	(1)	14.2	(3)	22.0	(2)	15.8	(2)	15.0	(1)
Inflation	6.8	(8)	19.3	(3)	15.7	(2)	16.6	(3)	9.4	(4)	10.0	(6)
Unemployment	10.6	(6)	14.1	(4)	9.0	(7)	12.0	(4)	7.5	(7)	11.9	(4)
Quebec Separatism	18.9	(3)	13.1	(5)	9.9	(5)	10.0	(6)	15.4	(3)	10.0	(6)
Domestic Gas & Oil Policy (including Petro-Can)	9.0	(7)	12.1	(6)	9.3	(6)	6.9	(8)	7.9	(6)	10.4	(5)
Tax Reform (including Mortgage Interest Plans)	4.7	(10)	11.4	(7)	11.0	(4)	8.1	(7)	2.3	(10)	5.8	(8)
Federal-Provincial Relations (non-separatism)	13.4	(5)	8.5	(9)	6.1	(8)	5.8	(9)	8.3	(5)	12.7	(3)
Television Debate	5.6	(9)	6.2	(10)	4.6	(9)	10.4	(5)	4.5	(9)	4.2	(9)
Economic Development	15.2	(4)	9.8	(8)	3.5	(10)	5.8	(9)	5.6	(8)	3.5	(10)

Table 3-2 — Percentage of Electoral Stories Dealing with Major Issues in the 1980 Campaign by TV and Radio Networks (with Rank Order)

NETWORK

CAMPAIGN ISSUE	TELEVISION								RADIO			
	CBC/FR (N=252)		CBC/ENG (N=205)		GLOBAL (N=170)		CTV (N=179)		RADIO CANADA (N=212)		CBC RADIO (N=209)	
	%	R/O	%	R/O	%	R/O	%	R/O	%	R/O	%	R/O
Leadership	36.9	(1)	37.1	(1)	28.8	(1)	41.3	(1)	17.0	(1)	24.9	(1)
Domestic Gas & Oil Policy	15.9	(2)	22.0	(2)	17.1	(3)	17.3	(4)	17.0	(1)	21.1	(2)
Iran	15.1	(3)	14.6	(4)	21.8	(2)	24.0	(2)	13.7	(3)	11.5	(5)
Polls	13.9	(4)	18.5	(3)	15.3	(5)	20.7	(3)	4.7	(8)	7.7	(9)
Conservative Budget	9.9	(6)	5.9	(10)	14.1	(6)	10.6	(8)	12.3	(4)	13.4	(4)
Canada–US Relations	5.6	(9)	8.8	(8)	17.1	(3)	12.3	(5)	4.7	(8)	9.6	(6)
Economic Development	11.1	(5)	9.3	(6)	6.5	(9)	10.6	(8)	6.1	(7)	8.6	(7)
Canada–USSR Relations	8.7	(7)	7.8	(9)	7.6	(8)	8.9	(10)	2.8	(10)	14.4	(3)
Tax Reform	4.4	(10)	9.3	(6)	10.6	(7)	11.2	(6)	8.0	(6)	7.7	(9)
Federal-Provincial Relations (non-separatism)	6.3	(8)	11.2	(5)	6.5	(9)	11.2	(6)	12.7	(5)	8.6	(7)

This is so, we would submit, because no party pushed its importance. The issue of Quebec separatism, which is a vital aspect of national unity, similarly faded from a position amongst the most important issues in 1980 as opposed to 1979. This is not because the issue had vanished; much to the contrary, it was still very important. But the media reported on what the political parties had to say, rather than on the underlying structural problems of the country. This emphasizes the degree to which parties control the subject matter of the campaign, if not its presentation. Our data indicate that, if political parties wish to stress short-term questions that will show them in a good light or discredit their opponents, they will be abetted in this by the media, who will not take it upon themselves to direct the attention of the public to the country's long-term structural problems.

The variation in the 1979 and 1980 agendas is also evident in the treatment of economic issues, particularly inflation and unemployment. In the first election, the Progressive Conservative opposition targeted on the charge of Liberal economic mismanagement, and this was also a theme of the New Democratic Party campaign. The amount of coverage accorded these topics reflected the success that they had in getting this message placed before the public. In 1980, however, inflation and unemployment, as separate issues in the economic realm, were not among the most frequently covered issues. The Progressive Conservatives in the 1980 campaign had a record — albeit a short one — to defend, and this revolved around the budget that had led to their defeat. Although their strategy was to continue to refer to the previous years of Liberal economic failure under Trudeau's leadership, the Liberals appeared successful in diverting reporting to the subject of the ineptness of the Conservative budget under Clark's leadership. The 1979 leader debate was not repeated in 1980, when commentary on poll results was the fourth-ranked topic of media coverage, buttressing Wilson's contention that journalists were engrossed with the "horserace" aspects of the election at the expense of substantive issues.[11]

When one looks for issues common to both election campaigns, four, besides leadership, emerge: domestic gas and oil policy, and economic development — both of which increase in importance in 1980 — and tax reform and federal-provincial relations — both of which garner less attention in 1980. Consequently, domestic gas and oil policy was a favored issue of the Liberal Party in 1979,[12] when they pushed the establishment and expansion of Petro-Canada, whereas the Progressive Conservatives proposed its "privatization." Petro-Canada was a newly developing oil exploration and refining Crown corporation that was rapidly becoming a competitor to private companies. The Liberal proposal was to expand the activities of Petro-Canada, while the PCs proposed that the Crown corporation be sold to private individuals and companies in the country. It later became clear that the PC proposal had met with very little public sympathy. In 1980, oil policy became even more salient as the Liberals attacked the proposed 18-cent-a-gallon excise tax on gasoline, which highlighted the Conservative budget. Domestic gas and oil policy became the second most reported issue in the 1980 election. Liberal proposals for an industrial strategy were responsible for a modest increase in attention given to economic development in 1980. Tax reform, centred around the Progressive Conservatives' mortgage interest deductibility plan, attracted continued commentary, although it received slightly less interest in 1980 than it had in 1979 when it was first proposed. Federal-provincial relations, and the respective abilities of the Progressive Conservatives and Liberals to deal effectively with provincial governments, remained on the list of top ten issues, but fell to last place among them in the 1980 campaign.

Five topics that were absent in 1979 emerged among the top ten in 1980. Three of these had do to with foreign policy: the Canadian role in rescuing American nationals from Iran, Canadian-American relations, and Canadian–Soviet Union relations. The latter two related to Soviet intervention in Afghanistan and the question of the appropriate responses to this action. These events raise an interesting question regarding media campaign coverage and political parties' attempts to direct the nature of this coverage: How do parties take advantage of extraneous events and turn them into opportunities for gain in their electoral strategy? Joe Clark's assertion that the Liberal–New Democratic Party defeat of his government was among the factors in the Soviets' decision to intervene in Afghanistan, in that it resulted in there being one less strong Western government to complain, was an attempt to highlight his party's tough anti-Soviet stance. Mr. Clark obviously would have liked the electorate to make such a momentous connection, but, after one passing attempt to encourage this line of thought, he dropped his argument. Of greater impact was the debate about what sanctions against the USSR, if any, were appropriate. These focused on options such as the Olympic boycott or various trade embargoes. Because President Carter had taken the lead in proposing retaliatory measures against the USSR, Canadian policy in this area was complicated by its impact on Canadian-American relations. Of even more importance was the potential for political gain for the PC government because of its role in the safe-keeping and eventual return home of American diplomatic personnel in Iran, made necessary by the seizure of the American embassy in Teheran. This issue certainly occupied the attention of the media, ranking third in overall coverage. The unaccustomed appearance of foreign policy issues on the election agenda was not the result of party decisions to give greater prominence to foreign policy during campaigns, but merely an attempt to take advantage of matters already in the public eye. The attention these issues attracted either meant that other domestic issues that might have appeared among the top ten were denied journalistic exposure, or that the domestic issues that were reported upon received less attention than otherwise might have been the case.

Finally, the Progressive Conservative budget was a new issue in 1980. Its importance is obvious as it was the catalyst that led to the call for an election in the first place. The budget is associated with other important issues, specifically domestic gas and oil policy and tax reform, and its handling also generated a significant amount of the commentary on leadership.

Table 3-3 — Percentage of Electoral Stories Dealing with Major Parties in 1979 and 1980, by TV and Radio Networks

NETWORK

	TELEVISION								RADIO			
	CBC/FR		CBC/ENG		GLOBAL		CTV		RADIO CANADA		CBC RADIO	
PARTY	1979 N=322	1980 N=252*	1979 N=306	1980 N=205	1979 N=345	1980 N=170	1979 N=259	1980 N=179	1979 N=266	1980 N=212	1979 N=260	1980 N=209
Liberal	51.6	51.2	51.0	58.5	56.2	52.4	56.4	44.7	43.2	55.2	41.5	45.9
Progressive Conservative	41.9	52.4	42.5	58.5	47.0	66.5	45.6	57.5	33.1	66.5	31.9	52.2
New Democratic Party	26.7	28.2	32.7	37.1	31.3	26.5	29.3	26.8	22.6	24.5	28.8	24.4
Social Credit/Raillement												
Créditiste	23.9	9.9	6.9	3.9	3.8	0.6	6.2	2.2	20.3	11.8	5.8	1.4
Parti Québecois	12.1	12.7	5.6	5.9	3.8	2.9	4.2	5.6	5.3	3.8	5.8	6.2

*N's cannot be compared directly as in 1980 we sampled broadcasts during the first few weeks of the campaign, while in 1979 all broadcasts were coded.

Party Coverage

While issues vary from election to election the political parties involved, with only rare exceptions, remain the same. Table 3-3 shows the percentage of electoral stories dealing with the major parties in the 1979 and 1980 elections. The most noteworthy feature of this table is the consistency with which all media organizations treated the parties in rough proportion to their strength in the House of Commons at dissolution. In 1979, without exception, the networks accorded the ruling Liberals greater attention than the official opposition by a nearly uniform 10% margin. There was more variation, however, in the treatment of the third-place NDP. For instance CBC English radio gave it only 2% less coverage than the PCs.

In 1980 the roles of the Liberal and Progressive Conservative parties reversed and so, nearly, did the relative attention paid to them by the electronic media. It was not, however, that the Liberals received dramatically less attention (except for CTV where the coverage represented an almost symmetrical reversal). In fact, a higher percentage of stories were devoted to them on the CBC English network and on Radio Canada. The major change in 1980 was the average 17% increase, across all six networks, of the coverage of the Progressive Conservatives. Still, coverage of the PCs in 1980, as the government party, did not exceed that of the Liberals to the same degree that coverage of the Liberals had exceeded coverage of the Conservatives in 1979. CBC English television treated them precisely equally, while CBC French television gave the governing party only a slight 1.2% edge. It may well be that the Liberals, especially as led by Mr. Trudeau, had not been out of office long enough to lose their attraction to media coverage. Nonetheless, it is clear from the huge increase in coverage of the PCs that the governing status of a party helps enormously in attracting media attention.

The relative position of the NDP remained unchanged in 1980 and there were no significant or unidirectional changes in coverage over the two elections. The Social Credit Party, however, experienced a significant loss of media interest in 1980, especially in the French media, which had accorded it only slightly less attention than the NDP in 1979. This decline in media coverage was parallelled by a similar response from the electorate, although no direct relationship is suggested here.

Mentions of the Parti Québecois, which at this time had not indicated an interest in federal politics, remained comparable with 1979 levels. An interesting organizational variation emerges, however, in the attention paid to the Parti Québecois by the CBC French television network as opposed to all other media organizations, including, significantly, Radio Canada in both 1979 and 1980. While we might have expected a consistency based on language, given the status of the PQ in Quebec, we find instead a difference clearly based on the kind of media organization. In this instance the amount of coverage was more affected by the complex of influences involved in the macro-gatekeeping function of a particular media network than by the common variable of French culture. Perhaps there is evidence here that might lend credence to Liberal charges of PQ influence on the French CBC network. However, those allegations extended to radio as well, so nothing conclusive can be drawn from our data on that question. It would be hard to argue that the PQ provided more visual impact and thus attracted more television coverage. The interest of French CBC television seems idiosyncratic, so its meaning is not derivable from our data.

Spearman Rank-Order Correlations

Tables 3-4 and 3-5 allow us to pursue further and with more precision the impact of not only media organization and language, but media type as well on election agenda. What these tables present is a measurement of similarity known as the Spearman Rank-order Correlation. This measurement compares rank orders, such as found in Tables 3-1 and 3-2, in such a way that if the agendas were perfectly matched, the Spearman Rank-order Correlation would be +1.0. On the other hand, if they were completely reversed, the resulting correlation would be -1.0. Correlations in the general area of 0 indicate no relationship between the rankings compared. Thus an examination of Tables 3-4 and 3-5 reveals that all these correlations are positive, the highest (+.84) being between CBC English television and CTV in 1980.

Table 3-4 — Spearman Rank-Order Correlation between all TV and Radio Network Agenda in the 1979 Campaign*

	CBC ENG	GLOBAL	CTV	RADIO CANADA	CBC/ENG RADIO
CBC/FR	.53	.25	.36	.79	.59
CBC/ENG	—	.82	.80	.75	.68
GLOBAL	—	—	.74	.65	.56
CTV	—	—	—	.67	.55
RADIO CANADA	—	—	—	—	.78

*all correlations are positive

Table 3-5 — Spearman Rank-Order Correlation between all TV and Radio Network Agenda in the 1980 Campaign*

	CBC ENG	GLOBAL	CTV	RADIO CANADA	CBC/ENG RADIO
CBC/FR	.70	.60	.61	.64	.61
CBC/ENG	—	.53	.84	.61	.23
GLOBAL	—	—	.83	.59	.54
CTV	—	—	—	.62	.24
RADIO CANADA	—	—	—	—	.56

*all correlations are positive

If one constructs a composite of all television network agenda and then calculates the Spearman Rank-order Correlation to a composite of the radio agenda, we arrive at a correlation of +.72 for 1979 and +.42 in 1980. If our composite agenda are based on language (English and French), the correlation produced in the first year is +.49 and +.70 in the second. Plainly, neither "gate" operated consistently to regulate the flow of information, with language accounting for greater variation in the 1979 election, while media type accounted for greater variation in 1980. In fact, however, it seems obvious that all three macro-gates were kept open to a broadly similar range of issues, and consequently it is possible to speak of a single "electronic media agenda" in both the 1979 and 1980 Canadian elections.

This is not to say that there were no variations at all. First, looking at 1979, we find a number of instances of marked dissimilarity in the linguistic-cultural agenda. Quebec separatism, as might be expected, elicited higher interest in the French-language media. Similarly, language-culture appears to create a consistent variation with respect to tax reform, inflation, federal-provincial relations, and economic development. The first two of these are ranked significantly lower on the composite French-language agenda than on the English one, while the second two are ranked considerably higher. As noted above, however, on coverage of the Parti Québecois, where there might have been an expectation of linguistic-cultural similarity, Radio Canada's coverage is closer to the English-language media than it is to CBC French television. However, the linguistic-cultural gate seems to be operative with respect to some other political parties, filtering out, for instance, material on the NDP, which has been electorally weak in Quebec (having never won a seat), and pushing to the fore material on the Raillement Créditiste, which is an electoral factor only in that province. On such a basis we do not believe it would be justified to speak of separate French and English media agendas, but we can perhaps more accurately speak of the existence of a "French variation" in the basic 1979 electronic media agenda. As indicated by the higher rank-order correlation between English and French agenda in 1980, there were less dramatic differences in coverage. These were accounted for by the French media's tendency to highlight questions dealing with federal-provincial relations, while at the same time covering Canadian-American relations less intensively.

Authors such as Siegel and Elkin have stressed the differences between English and French media and the existence of different linguistic news agendas.[13] Our findings, while showing some evidence of linguistic-cultural differences, run counter to these studies, in that the variations are less noteworthy than are the similarities. From this we may conclude that national elections are, broadly speaking, integrating events and their reporting by the news media does not run counter to that function.

Finally, in terms of comparative radio and television coverage of the campaigns, in 1979 the overall rank-order correlation between the two composite agendas was quite high. With respect to specific issues, radio paid more attention to federal-provincial relations and less to tax reform than did television. In 1980, however, it was media type that produced a

Table 3-6 — Percentage of Electoral Stories (over three minutes in length) Dealing with Major Parties and Issues by TV and Radio Networks (1979 and 1980 Data)

NETWORK

| | TELEVISION | | | | | | | | RADIO | | | |
| | CBC/FR | | CBC/ENG | | GLOBAL | | CTV | | RADIO CANADA | | CBC RADIO | |
	1979	1980	1979	1980	1979	1980	1979	1980	1979	1980	1979	1980
Liberal	10.9	2.3	7.0	14.2	6.2	6.0	4.0	6.3	3.5	6.0	16.8	3.1
Progressive Conservative	12.6	1.5	7.4	12.5	5.6	4.7	1.9	4.9	2.9	4.3	19.3	3.7
New Democratic Party	12.8	2.8	7.5	14.5	5.2	7.0	1.5	6.3	4.3	3.9	22.7	5.9
Leadership	12.8	1.1	5.4	10.5	10.1	6.7	6.0	5.4	0	5.7	24.3	3.8
Domestic Gas & Oil Policy	13.8	0	15.2	22.2	13.0	7.4	12.5	12.9	0	5.6	3.7	6.8
Economic Development	20.4	0	14.8	5.3	0	0	0	10.5	0	0	11.1	0
Tax Reform	40.0	9.1	0	31.6	2.9	27.8	10.0	5.0	16.7	11.8	13.3	0
Fed.-Prov. Relations	14.0	0	4.5	17.4	11.8	9.1	7.1	10.0	0	3.7	18.2	0
National Unity	9.7		10.8		4.9		5.9		0		20.5	
Quebec Separatism	8.2		14.3		7.1		0		2.9		30.8	
Inflation	31.8		13.2		7.3		7.3		13.6		7.7	
Unemployment	26.5		17.5		4.0		6.9		10.0		16.1	
Iran		5.3		13.3		2.8		2.3		3.6		16.7
Polls		2.9		18.4		19.2		13.5		0		0
Cons. Budget		4.0		25.0		13.6		5.3		11.5		3.6
Canada-US Relations		0		22.2		3.7		4.5		0		10.0
Canada-USSR Relations		0		12.5		7.7		6.3		0		0

wider variation in the intensity of coverage devoted to various issues. Television accentuated the issues of Iran and Canadian-American relations, while radio emphasized federal-provincial relations and Canadian-Soviet relations. From this we conclude simply that while each medium may on occasion, for reasons of its own, choose to emphasize one issue or another, there is little by way of consistent patterns in such choices. Television, of course, will always be attracted to issues and events that provide the opportunity for a strong visual impact, but cannot ignore news where such is not the case.

Length of Story

Another aspect of media coverage that merits comment has to do with the time length of the story. We assume that the length of time accorded to a news item is a reflection of the importance of that story in the opinion of those who put together newscasts. Table 3-6 shows the percentage of stories dealing with each theme that were over three minutes long. These data, however, can only be appreciated fully when analyzed in conjunction with the data in Tables 3-1, 3-2, and 3-3, because the lengthier news items may represent a high percentage of relatively few stories, while an absence of lengthy stories does not mean that an issue was not covered in many shorter segments. With these qualifications in mind, it is indisputable that making over three minutes of air time available to a particular item is an important gatekeeping decision.

Looking first at the coverage of the major parties, it is apparent that neither language nor media type provides the chief basis for variation. For instance, CBC English television ran a higher percentage of long stories on all parties in 1980, whereas CBC English radio evidenced a dramatic trend in the opposite direction. Similarly, CBC French television and Radio Canada moved in different directions. Thus language provided no prediction of consistency in the length of news items. The same inconsistency is revealed if one looks at both CBC television networks, as opposed to the two CBC radio networks. Unquestionably, individual news production teams themselves were the most significant factor in determining the length of news stories about political parties.

An interesting observation that emerges from Table 3-6 is that the premier coverage afforded to the governing party that was noted in our earlier discussion does not apply in terms of lengthy stories. Thus in 1980, in comparison with the other parties, the Progressive Conservatives' share of prolonged attention actually decreased, while the Liberals, and even more so the NDP, increased their percentage of long stories. This was true of all media, and while not easily interpreted, it does mitigate the favored position of the governing party strongly suggested by earlier analysis.

When we turn to the issues of the two campaigns, however, there is evidence of different treatment in terms of length of stories by the two media language groups. In 1979 on French-language radio and television, a larger proportion of tax reform stories occupied three or more minutes than was the case for any other issue. They were similarly in agreement about inflation being second and unemployment third as worthy of lengthy airtime. An "English agenda" is less coherent, but it is perhaps worth noting that two of the three English television networks rated gas and oil policy most favorably for extended treatment, while with the third network it was a close second. CBC radio did not follow suit. On the other end of the scale, CBC television, Global TV, and CBC radio all gave tax reform very little extended exposure. This time, CTV played the role of the maverick.

In 1980, patterns are less definite. French-language organizations are still in agreement on the primacy of tax reform, but now CBC English television and Global TV have joined them. The English media continue to exhibit a slight tendency to give more lengthy treatment to the gas and oil policy issue than the French. The significance of these patterns should not be overemphasized, but they are suggestive enough to warrant testing in future research.

While the data do not provide the basis for clear answers as to why there is variation (or consistency for that matter) in the length of time accorded to certain kinds of stories, we are prepared to speculate, at least with regard to political parties. There, the doctrine of journalistic fairness, as applied to the electronic media, is normally arrived at by providing time to the major parties based on their representation in Parliament. The media experts of the political parties closely monitor the performance of radio and television on this score, and while the equal time doctrine is not mandated for news broadcasts as it is for free-time broadcasts, it is nevertheless a convention of journalistic practice. The provision of occasional lengthy stories, concentrating on one or another political party, may well be a mechanism by which the networks achieve the balance, which may be less possible to do on a daily basis.

Story Placement

Another variable that sheds light on the concept of agenda-setting is the place accorded to a story in the news program sequence. Table 3-7 shows for each theme the percentage of news stories that appeared in the lead position in network broadcasts.

Applying this criterion to political party stories, we find less unanimity in percentages of lead story status than was the case in Table 3-1, which depicted the rank order of parties by total story mentions. This generalization holds true for both elections. We may note, for example, that in 1979, while CTV had fewer news stories dealing with the PCs than with the Liberals, a slightly higher percentage of those PC stories were accorded lead status. Similarly, both CBC English television and radio networks slotted a larger percentage of their NDP stories (albeit these were a smaller absolute number) into the lead position than they did for the PC party.

Table 3-7 — Percentage of Electoral Stories (in the lead position) Dealing with Major Parties and Issues by TV and Radio Networks (1979 and 1980 Data)

	NETWORK											
	TELEVISION								RADIO			
	CBC/FR		CBC/ENG		GLOBAL		CTV		RADIO CANADA		CBC RADIO	
	1979	1980	1979	1980	1979	1980	1979	1980	1979	1980	1979	1980
Liberal	9.0	5.4	12.9	5.0	8.9	6.8	10.3	11.3	11.3	2.6	5.6	5.2
Progressive Conservative	7.4	4.5	8.5	7.5	7.5	10.7	11.0	12.6	9.2	5.7	3.6	3.7
New Democratic Party	7.0	4.2	12.0	3.9	5.7	4.4	9.2	10.4	5.1	2.0	4.0	3.9
Leadership	4.7	3.2	8.6	5.3	8.1	6.1	9.6	8.1	4.2	2.9	2.7	3.8
Domestic Gas & Oil Policy	6.9	0	10.8	2.2	15.6	3.4	27.8	9.7	9.5	5.6	7.4	0
Economic Development	2.0	0	13.3	0	16.7	0	13.5	10.5	6.7	0	0	0
Tax Reform	6.7	9.1	11.4	0	5.4	11.1	19.0	10.0	16.7	5.9	0	0
Fed.-Prov. Relations	4.7	0	0	4.3	23.8	9.1	20.0	10.0	4.5	0	6.1	0
National Unity	6.9		12.2		16.7		15.8		11.9		2.6	
Quebec Separatism	1.6		12.5		14.7		20.0		2.4		3.8	
Inflation	4.5		8.5		13.0		7.0		0		3.8	
Unemployment	11.8		11.6		13.8		3.2		5.0		0	
Iran		15.8		16.7		13.5		16.3		10.7		25.0
Polls		14.3		5.3		11.5		13.5		0		6.3
Cons. Budget		4.0		0		8.7		5.3		0		0
Canada-US Relations		7.1		11.1		13.8		13.6		22.2		15.0
Canada-USSR Relations		0		6.3		0		6.3		16.7		6.7

In 1980, political parties in general garnered a smaller percentage of lead stories. This trend, evident everywhere but on CTV, is particularly dramatic for the Liberal and New Democratic parties. The magnitude of Liberal decline in this aspect of reporting is most noticeable on the two French-language networks.

Turning our attention to some substantive issues, we find some interesting variations from the 1979 rank-order data. For example, the 1979 French-language agenda gave greater prominence in terms of frequency of mention to the issues of Quebec separatism, federal-provincial relations, and economic development, but in terms of placement in the news broadcast, we do not see evidence of an attempt to highlight these issues.

The difference between measuring media salience by rank ordering the frequency of mention of stories and the measure focusing on the sequence of the story in the newscast is most vividly shown by an examination of CTV's 1979 treatment of the leadership issue and the issue of domestic gas and oil policy. In absolute numbers, leadership occupied first place on CTV's agenda, with 75 total stories, yet only 7 of these, or 9.6%, were lead stories. By way of contrast, domestic gas and oil policy merited only 18 total stories. However, 5 of these, or 27.8%, led off the newscasts. This same phenomenon is exhibited by the Global network with respect to leadership and federal-provincial relations.

In the 1980 agenda, the percentage of lead stories dealing with leadership falls off consistently, except for CBC radio, where a modest increase is noted. The issue of domestic gas and oil registers an even more severe decline, most noticeable on CTV, where it had been very prominent in 1979. What appears to have happened in 1980 is that the Iranian situation and a number of international events often garnered the lead story status on all networks during the campaign period. Surprisingly, given that it precipitated the election, the Conservative budget did not merit lead story status to any great extent.

The electronic media have to contend with a variety of competing distractions, ranging from dinner for the radio news we were monitoring, to bedtime in the case of the network television newscasts. People have acquired the habit of devoting full attention to the first few items on a newscast before drifting off to other activities. Indeed, newscasts often begin with comments such as "Leading off the news tonight is..." or "The top story in tonight's news is..." In light of this, according lead story status to a news item magnifies its importance by some unknown, though certainly significant, factor.

The ability of a political party during an election campaign to have issues that they feel are working for them highlighted on the electronic media is reflected in the number of leads these issues are accorded in news broadcasts. Therefore, an assessment of who has won a media campaign must take the question of placement into account. No consistent pattern on lead story status appears in our data. However, if any future study were to reflect one party or one issue dominating in number of lead stories, it would indeed be a significant finding.

Evaluation of Party Leaders

While agenda-setting theory itself does not focus on the evaluative dimension, it is apparent that networks, in setting their agendas, are either unable or unwilling to avoid presentation of material that can be viewed as portraying leaders and parties favorably or unfavorably. In terms of coding criteria, stories were judged to be either positive or negative when they were obviously favorable or unfavorable to a party, its policies, or its leaders.

In this regard, Table 3-8 portrays the percentage of stories which included comments on major party leaders in the two election campaigns. In 1979 the data reveal a strongly negative direction in the commentary pertaining to Trudeau and Clark, although this negative tendency is less emphatic with respect to radio. For Trudeau, the percentage of stories containing a negative orientation varied from a low of 3.4% on Radio Canada to a high of 11.2% on CBC French television. For Clark, we find a low in negative comments of 4.1%, again on Radio Canada, to a high of 12.7% on CTV. In contrast, the percentage of positively oriented stories on Trudeau varied from a high of 4.2% on CTV to a low of 2.6% on both radio networks. Clark enjoyed most favorable treatment at the hands of CBC English television, where 2.6% of stories were favorable to him. Global television gave him fewest positive stories, only 1.4%. Broadbent, while receiving less coverage overall (and therefore less salience in terms of agenda-setting theory), was the object of more favorable commentary than negative on four of the six media networks (CTV, Global, and both radio networks), and only slightly more negative commentary on the two CBC television networks. CTV accorded him both the most positive and the most negative treatment (3.9% and 2.3% respectively). Fabien Roy and René Lévesque received too little evaluative commentary to merit comment, and are included in the table only because of Roy's leadership status and Lévesque's direct connection with the major issues of national unity and Quebec separatism.

In 1980, we see that the negative tendency toward Trudeau is continued from the 1979 election. However, it is less intense on some networks while more concentrated on others, peaking at 12.2% on the CBC English television network, a higher percentage than appeared anywhere in 1979. Positive commentary on the Liberal leader increased marginally on both CBC televison networks, as well as on CTV and CBC radio.

For the most part, the amount of negative commentary on Clark fell in 1980, most dramatically on CTV. The exceptions to this trend were Global television and CBC radio, the latter showing a decidedly more negative stance. The percentage of positive commentary on Clark was higher in 1980 on all networks, with the exception of Radio Canada. Increases, however, were for the most part marginal.

In 1980 there was no consistent pattern of increase or decrease in negative commentary on Broadbent. The largest increase occurred on Global, while the decreases were all rather marginal. With positive commentary, we also see a lack of consistency in the trends. The most significant single change is the drop to zero in the case of CTV, as compared to 3.9% in

Table 3-8 — Percentage of Electoral Stories Reflecting Positively or Negatively on Major Party Leaders, by TV and Radio Networks (1979 and 1980 Data)

NETWORK

| | | CBC/FR 1979/N=322 1980/N=252 | | CBC/ENG 1979/N=306 1980/N=205 | | GLOBAL 1979/N=345 1980/N=170 | | CTV 1979/N=259 1980/N=179 | | RADIO CANADA 1979/N=266 1980/N=212 | | CBC RADIO 1979/N=260 1980/N=209 | |
		POS.	NEG.	POS.	NEG.	POS.	NEG.	POS.	NEG.	POS.	NEG.	POS.	NEG.
Trudeau	1979	3.1	11.2	2.6	9.5	3.8	6.7	4.2	8.5	2.3	3.4	2.3	4.6
	1980	4.0	5.6	3.9	12.2	3.5	4.7	4.5	10.1	0.5	0.9	3.3	6.2
Clark	1979	1.6	7.1	2.6	8.2	1.4	6.4	1.5	12.7	2.3	4.1	1.5	4.2
	1980	4.4	4.4	3.9	6.3	1.8	7.1	2.2	3.9	0.5	0	1.9	10.0
Broadbent	1979	0.9	1.6	0.9	1.6	1.5	0.3	3.9	2.3	1.9	0.4	1.9	0.4
	1980	1.2	1.2	2.0	2.4	0	1.8	0	1.7	0	0	1.0	0
Roy	1979	1.2	0.6	1.2	0.6	0	0.9	0.4	0.4	0.4	0	0	0
	1980	0.4	0	0	0.5	0	0.9	0	0	0	0	0	0.5
Lévesque	1979	0	0.6	0	0.7	0.3	0.3	0	0.4	0	0	0	0
	1980	0.4	1.6	0	0	0	0.6	0	0.6	0	0	0	0.5

1979. Neither Roy nor Lévesque evoked much of an evaluative response from the media in the 1980 election.

Thus in summary we see that in both elections all six media organizations commented in an obviously negative manner on the leaders of the two major parties, except for the French television and radio networks in 1980, where positive and negative commentary were virtually the same for Mr. Clark. Whereas in 1979, Mr. Broadbent of the NDP received more positive commentary than negative, in 1980 his pattern of evaluation was more congruent with that of the two major party leaders.

Much of this negative commentary derived from the fact that the networks chose to highlight the attacks of the party leaders on each other. In doing so, they were acting as conduits of the parties' campaign strategy, but their choice fits well with the conflict-oriented trend that the media seem to prefer. It seems probable that Broadbent was the subject of less negative commentary because Clark and Trudeau concentrated on attacking each other rather than the minority party leader.

Evaluation of Political Parties

In their presentation of political parties in 1979, the six media organizations included material that was likely to evoke reactions from viewers. In the case of both major parties and their leaders, the likely impact would be negative. This pattern is repeated in 1980, with the exception of the CBC French television network, which accorded the Liberal Party somewhat more positive treatment.

In 1979, the NDP was cast in a positive more often than in a negative light, the only party to be so portrayed, and by all six media organizations. This ceased to be the case in 1980, except for CBC radio. In 1979 the CBC English television network was highly negative toward the Liberals, with 17.3% of its stories judged to be negative in orientation. This tendency was even more pronounced in 1980 when 22.5% of this network's stories dealing with the Liberals had a negative focus, combined with a smaller percentage of positive evaluations. While in 1979 Radio Canada followed closely, with 16.3% of its stories portraying the Liberals negatively, in the 1980 election this fell off dramatically, when only 3.3% of its stories on the Liberals were negative. In 1979 the Progressive Conservative party was treated negatively in 11.7% of CTV stories, while its most positive treatment came at the hands of Global (8.4%). In 1980 Global continued to have the highest percentage of positive evaluations of the Progressive Conservatives. However, this was combined with the highest negative commentary. The result of this for Global is a more negative balance of commentary in the second campaign. This was a part of an overall deterioration in the balance of positive and negative commentary dealing with the PCs in 1980, with positive comments falling slightly and negative ones increasing substantially. In 1979 CBC English television accorded the NDP both its most positive and negative treatments, 6.9% and 4% respectively. In 1980, CBC radio gave the NDP its highest percentage of positive evaluation (4.3%), while CBC English

Table 3-9 — Percentage of Electoral Stories Reflecting Positively or Negatively on Major Parties, Their Policies, or Personnel, by TV and Radio Networks (1979 and 1980 Data)

NETWORK

		TELEVISION								RADIO			
		CBC/FR 1979/N=322 1980/N=252		CBC/ENG 1979/N=306 1980/N=205		GLOBAL 1979/N=345 1980/N=170		CTV 1979/N=259 1980/N=179		RADIO CANADA 1979/N=266 1980/N=212		CBC RADIO 1979/N=260 1980/N=209	
		POS.	NEG.	POS.	NEG.	POS.	NEG.	POS.	NEG.	POS.	NEG.	POS.	NEG.
Liberal	1979	4.7	14.0	5.9	17.3	6.4	14.9	8.8	12.0	1.9	16.3	5.0	13.9
	1980	5.2	3.6	4.9	22.5	4.7	18.2	3.9	16.2	1.4	3.3	5.8	12.0
PC	1979	1.5	9.0	7.9	11.4	8.4	10.2	7.3	11.7	4.9	8.7	4.6	5.4
	1980	2.8	5.2	7.8	15.2	10.0	20.0	6.1	16.8	1.4	6.6	2.9	17.3
NDP	1979	1.9	1.2	6.9	4.0	4.4	3.2	6.6	3.1	4.5	2.3	4.6	2.0
	1980	0	0.8	3.9	4.5	1.2	4.2	1.7	4.5	0.5	0.5	4.3	2.4
SC/RC	1979	0.6	0.6	1.0	1.6	0	2.9	0.4	0.8	0.8	1.2	0	0
	1980	1.2	0	0	1.5	0	0.6	0	0.6	0	0.5	0	0.5
PQ	1979	0.3	0.9	0	1.3	0	2.6	0.4	1.6	0.4	0.8	0	1.9
	1980	0.4	1.6	0	2.5	0	1.8	0	0.6	0	1.4	0	3.3

television and CTV tied with the highest percentage of negative stories, (4.5%). On the dimension of the directional commentary regarding political parties over two elections, there do not appear to be differences based either on language-culture or media type.

The negativism that characterized both of these campaigns appears to be a characteristic of the electronic media, regardless of language, media type, or network. We will discuss the implications of this on the political process in the concluding chapter.

Conclusions

The news output of four television and two radio networks during two eight-week election campaigns cannot be assumed to be representative behavior of these networks. Election campaigns are periods of heightened political debate, and a search for "typical" media behavior would necessitate studying media over a lengthy period not encompassing a national election. The conclusions that we can offer here about gatekeeping and agenda-setting are therefore limited to the electoral environment.

With regard to the three macro-gates that we identified earlier, organization, language-culture, and media type, it appears that the six media organizations responded to party electoral strategies in a generally similar manner. It is also evident that, notwithstanding some obvious differences between the French-language and English-language agendas in 1979, our data over two elections support the view that there in fact existed one national electronic media agenda rather than two separate agendas based on language differences. This conclusion is bolstered by the evaluative material on the major parties and their leaders, in which all the networks shared a common, critical style.

Our judgment on the performance of the electronic media in the context of the two elections is that Canadians receiving their news from different electronic media outlets were presented with similar pictures of the campaigns. The reasons for this homogeneity are not completely clear, nor is there a universally accepted answer to the question of whether it should be a cause for satisfaction or concern. These similarities in coverage have at least three potential explanations: (1) collusion between the various networks (we rule this out); (2) a manifestation of the kind of pack journalism described by Timothy Crouse in his book, The Boys on the Bus,[14] and detected as well by Clive Cocking in his treatment of the 1979 Canadian campaign;[15] or (3) that the major party campaign strategies of stressing various issues and leadership was more or less successful, in that the press rather faithfully reported what the politicians were saying, rather than attempting to develop and highlight a rival press agenda for the elections. With regard to the advantages and disadvantages of this less than forceful instance of gatekeeping on the part of the electronic media, much can be said.

Politicians and political parties give play to those issues that they believe will work for them and studiously avoid those that they see as problematic. On the one hand, it is the responsibility of the media to give adequate coverage to the variety of issues that different parties emphasize, rather than to be beguiled by their own concept of what is newsworthy or important. Thus if there is implicit agreement among politicians about what the salient issues are, do the media have any credentials to legitimate an attempt to set an alternative agenda? On the other hand, one of the functions of the media in a democratic society is to put the hard questions to politicians (despite their attempts to avoid them) and to report what is not said as well as what is said. In this sense, our data tend to characterize the electronic media as holding the fiddle for the politicians to play, rather than attempting to call the tune.

While the negative implications of this gatekeeping stance are very real, there may be some advantages to this style of coverage. In a country such as Canada, with its strong linguistic and regional cleavages, we see the electronic media as playing an unplanned rather than a conscious integrative role. We cannot detect a conscious effort on the part of the electronic media to comply with the mandate of the Broadcasting Act to promote the national interest, or, on the part of the CBC networks specifically, to foster national unity.[16] However, by the mere fact that the media tended to report on the same set of basic issues and picked up the evaluation of the campaign in a similar tone, we believe that this resultant electronic media output worked to provide diverse groups of Canadians with a unified picture of the political problems facing the country and the likelihood that major parties and politicians could be successful in dealing with these problems.[17]

We suspect that this homogeneity may be due, at least in part, to the physical presence of the networks in Toronto and Montreal. This tends to give a central Canadian bias to the events, issues, and personalities considered important in the campaign. While it is true that the electronic media follow national political leaders from coast to coast and report on their comments about regional issues, we hypothesize they concentrate on aspects of the campaign that are thought to be of interest to a national audience that is, in the majority, situated in central Canada.[18]

This chapter has sought to expand on the view that the gatekeeping process and the news agenda it produces are not simply the results of conscious individual decisions of news gatherers and disseminators. Rather they are the end results of a very broad and inclusive system in which culture, institutional organization, and technological capacity provide a framework in which some decisions are more likely than others.

The basic question, therefore, is: how much influence is exercised by the macro- and micro-gates in the preparation of the news? In the instance of the behavior of electronic media in the 1979 and 1980 Canadian federal elections, we are not yet sure that a clear relationship exists between the gates and differentiation in the selection and portrayal of issues. Nonetheless, the constraints that form a part of the gatekeeping process certainly can be argued to have had some impact.

Notes

[1]Harold D. Clarke, Jane Jenson, Lawrence LeDuc, and Jon Pammett, *Political Choice in Canada* (Toronto: McGraw-Hill-Ryerson, 1979), pp. 361-5. See also by the same authors, "Change in the Garden: The 1979 Election," paper presented to the annual meeting of the Canadian Political Science Association, Montreal, 1980, pp. 3-6.

[2]W. L. White, R. H. Wagenberg, and R. C. Nelson, *Introduction to Canadian Politics and Government*, 2nd ed. (Toronto: Holt, Rinehart and Winston of Canada, 1977), p. 89.

[3]William O. Gilsdorf, "Getting the Message Across: The Communication Strategy of the Federal Liberal Party in the 1979 and 1980 Canadian Federal Elections," paper presented to the annual meeting of the Canadian Communication Association, Université du Québec à Montréal, 1980.

[4]Frederick J. Fletcher, "The Mass Media in the 1974 Canadian Election," in Howard R. Penniman, ed., *Canada at the Polls: The General Election of 1974* (Washington: American Enterprise Institute for Public Policy Research,1975), pp. 253-4.

[5]Jeremy Wilson, "Media Coverage of Canadian Election Campaigns: Horserace Journalism and the Meta-Campaign," *Journal of Canadian Studies,* 15 (Winter 1980-1981), pp. 60-1.

[6]Walter C. Soderlund and Ronald H. Wagenberg, "The Editor and External Affairs: The 1972 and 1974 Election Campaigns," *International Journal*, 11 (Spring 1976), pp. 244-54.

[7]See in this regard: Frederick Elkin, "Communications Media and Identity Formation in Canada," in Benjamin Singer, ed., *Communications in Canadian Society* (Toronto: Copp Clark, 1972), pp. 222-3; Arthur Siegel, "Canadian Newspaper Coverage of the F.L.Q. Crisis: A Study on the Impact of the Press on Politics," (Ph.D. Dissertation, McGill University, 1974); and Arthur Siegel, "French and English Broadcasting in Canada—A Political Evaluation," *Canadian Journal of Communication*, 5 (Winter 1979), pp. 1-17.

[8]Gildsdorf, pp. 6-13.

[9]Ibid., pp. 13-4.

[10]Harold D. Clarke, Jane Jensen, Lawrence LeDuc, and Jon Pammett, "Voting Behavior and the Outcome of the 1979 Federal Election: The Impact of Leaders and Issues," *Canadian Journal of Political Science*, XV (September, 1982), pp. 517-52. See especially Tables 3, 4, and 11.

[11]Wilson, pp. 65-7.

[12]Gilsdorf, pp. 14-5.

[13]The studies by Siegel and Elkin are referred to in footnote 7. For information on alleged media bias, see *Committee of Inquiry into the National Broadcasting Service Report* (Ottawa: CRTC, July 1977.)

[14]Timothy Crouse, *The Boys on the Bus* (New York: Ballantine Books, 1974), pp.7-15.

[15]Clive Cocking, *Following the Leaders: A Media Watcher's Diary of Campaign '79* (Toronto: Doubleday, 1980), p. 106.

[16]The Canadian broadcasting system is mandated in this manner: "the Canadian broadcasting system should be effectively owned and controlled by Canadians so as to safeguard, enrich, and strengthen the cultural, political, social and economic fabric of Canada;" and in the case of the Canadian

Broadcasting Corporation, to "contribute to the development of national unity and provide for a continuing expression of Canadian identity." See Canada, *Broadcasting Act 1968* (Ottawa: Queen's Printer, 1968), Part I, 2, (b) and (g). Thus while we are not able to detect a direct causal link between this mandate and the selection of issues, nonetheless, because of the legal constraints, which form a part of the gatekeeping process as we have defined the term, it can be seen how regulation of this kind might well influence news selection.

[17]For an extended discussion of this point, see R. H. Wagenberg, W. C. Soderlund, E. D. Briggs, and W. I. Romanow, "Media Agenda-Setting in the 1979 Canadian Federal Election: Some Implication for Political Support," in Allan Kornberg and Harold D. Clarke, eds., *Political Support in Canada: The Crisis Years* (Durham: Duke University Press, 1983).

[18]This hypothesis is presently being investigated by William O. Gilsdorf.

4

Newspaper Reporting of the 1979 Campaign

As the early pages of this book indicated, the newspaper in Canada has a long and integral connection with the electoral process. Today, however, while their role is still significant, they have to share the field with the electronic media, and people who work on newspapers sometimes feel that they have been elbowed to the sidelines, especially by the upstart television. Such a concern may well have developed from a recently apparent trend in distribution of advertising dollars to different media in the country. Net advertising revenues of newspapers, for example, dropped by nearly 5% between 1972 and 1980, while those of television increased by about the same amount. Newspapers continue to reap more advertising dollars than any other medium in the country, but this position of dominance is no longer assured.[1]

This situation is not without its ironies. Among other things, those who owned newspapers found radio stations to be attractive additions to their corporate holdings from the very beginning. This multimedia ownership, or cross-ownership, as it is sometimes called, is a contemporary phenomenon as well, and is a cause for concern among students of communications and the democratic process.[2]

Beyond the question of ownership the style of journalism introduced by the electronic media has been derided by the craftspeople of the print media. Radio introduced, and television magnified, presentational elements of reporting, such as a good voice and appearance, that print journalists regarded as having little to do with the substance of politics on which their professional responsibilities centred. Indeed, the role of the reporter in the electronic media is often perceived as less significant than in the newspaper world. David Halberstam, for instance, argues that crucial news-gathering decisions in television are made by producers and that reporters are merely "talent" asigned to cover a particular story, like actors engaged to perform a set piece. According to Halberstam, producerism is a system in which the producers of a news show controlled the news, in which the public relations man for a government office or a senator's office could call the producer, not the correspondent, outline the story, explain the film possibility, and have the producer pencil in the story on the assignment sheet, often with the notation: "Talent to be assigned." *Talent to be assigned.* Which was a complete reversal of the traditional journalistic procedure of the correspondent wending his way through the field, using his eyes and ears and sensing what is important, what is a story, and then telling the home office.[3]

Nevertheless, newspaper reporters have had to swallow the bitter new reality that those less imbued with the "true" traditions of journalism are the ones sought out by politicians aspiring to gain public exposure.

This change in the pecking order in the journalistic fraternity did not happen instantaneously with the arrival of the electronic media. Those who operated the new technology had to develop and refine their craft, while politicians had to realize the potential for political gain now available to them through these new avenues of access to the electorate. Thus, as described earlier, it wasn't until the 1930s that radio was fully exploited for political purposes. Similarly, the early years of television did not indicate the overwhelming importance that it was later to assume in political life.

It seems in retrospect to be appropriate that John F. Kennedy, the good-looking, modern standard-bearer of the intellectual and progressive forces of the eastern seaboard of the United States, was among the earliest beneficiaries of the potential of television.[4] Less immediately apparent is the advantage that John Diefenbaker, the prairie lawyer and the defender of traditionalism in social issues, garnered from the new medium in Canada. The visual impact each leader could make in his own way need not be related to any particular kind of message. The evangelical zeal of John Diefenbaker and the good looks and style of John Kennedy simply could not be transmitted through the newspaper, even when accompanied by pictures, with the same impact as television could provide. Moreover, the contrast with less attractive opponents, who made for uninspiring viewing, served to heighten the advantage. Clive Cocking and William Gilsdorf, both of whom travelled with the press corps in the 1979-1980 campaigns, refer to the paramount status of television and the consequent grousing on the part of print journalists.[5]

While most would concede that television has become the dominant political/electoral medium, newspapers are not without their place. There is an analogy between the new electronic empire and its traditional precursor, the newspaper, with that of the Roman Empire and her subject state of Greece. For just as Rome continued to pay respect to the intellectual and cultural heritage of Greece, despite the subservient political role of the latter country, so does television continue to take serious heed of the substance of newspaper reporting.

While newspapers have been moving toward a more entertainment-oriented approach, they remain for the most part a medium devoted to providing information and opinion. The rise of tabloid newspapers in many of Canada's major cities can be considered evidence of an even more concentrated effort by publishers to imitate what is attracting people. Television, of course, remains overwhelmingly a vehicle for entertainment, much to the disappointment of many who see for it more serious potential. The entertainment ethic invades public affairs broadcasting and even the presentation of the news itself. This allows newspapers to retain the mantle of the serious information medium. As a result, those most interested in following political events have retained their loyalty to the newspaper as a purveyor of contemporary items of interest. Among those who regularly read the newspapers are the people who are responsible for preparing and delivering the television news, and the importance that newspapers attach to events may in fact have an impact on the gatekeeping and agenda-setting roles of television.[6]

Newspapers are journals of opinion as well as information. Through their editorials, columnists (some of whom are widely syndicated), even letters to the editor, they give vent to the expression of ideas in ways that television has largely avoided. The introduction of radio talk shows has provided an electronic approximation of the letter to the editor, but their primary purpose is still entertainment rather than reasoned argument. In any event, by the 1970s politicians had mastered the talk show format, and were able to use them for their own political advantage. Newspapers, it must be remembered, are under no legal or even conventional obligation to provide balance in their presentation of opinion, although they would claim to do so in straight news reporting, especially during elections. Television and radio are more circumspect in this regard. Politicians are permitted to deliver their own opinions, over the air waves, balanced by the right of reply on the part of their adversaries.

It is to newspapers, therefore, that politicians and opinion leaders will turn to gauge reaction to public policies. Questions in the House of Commons are more likely to find their genesis in the print media. The angle that is chosen for particular stories on television is often similarly conditioned by newspaper cues. That this should be the case, even in the face of wider public acceptance of the reliability of television, is indeed an irony.[7] Newspapers retain the ability to provide the in-depth, intensive coverage of news stories for which television newscasts are not suited. Television can convey immediacy and mood through its visual technology, but it cannot easily convey historical, social, or cultural contexts in the amount of time allocated to news broadcasts. Complex ideas and arguments are hardly suited to, at best, a three-minute news item, let alone a thirty-second clip. Thus for the serious consumer of public affairs information, the newspaper has remained indispensable.

The newspaper also remains easier to use. One can turn at one's convenience directly to items of interest without having to move sequentially through the pages. While retention of television programming through video taping is now widespread, it is a process much more complex (and expensive) than scanning yesterday's newspaper.

For those whose interest in the news is less intense the newspaper has lost much of its usefulness. Television and radio are normally able to

place contemporary news before the public more quickly than newspapers. It is only through investigative reporting to develop stories that
newspapers retain any capacity to beat the other media in the race to be
first with the news.[8]

Thus newspapers find themselves in an uncomfortable position. Despite their ability to convey a very much larger amount of information
than their television counterparts, they have lost much of their appeal to
segments of the population who would have been their readers in previous years. Even their attempts to adopt norms associated with the entertainment orientation of television have not reversed this trend and in
fact may have undermined their credibility with those who continue to
seek more serious treatment of the news. Despite these problems newspapers have continued to make an impact on the agenda that confronts
the public, both in ordinary periods and during election campaigns.

The Kent Commission Report

In the face of the relative decline of the newspapers' influence as television came to rule the roost, the appointment of the Kent Royal Commission to probe the operation of the industry might have been seen by
newspaper owners as adding insult to injury. Nonetheless, there had
been growing agitation among observers of the newspaper medium
about the concentration of ownership as chains acquired independently
owned newspapers. This concern increased in Canada when one chain
acquired another. Finally, when two major newspapers were closed by
their corporate owners on the same day, thereby eliminating competition in Ottawa and Winnipeg, the government was moved to act and the
Royal Commission on Newspapers came into being on September 3, 1980.

The Kent Commission was mandated to look into how the increased
concentration of ownership and the decreased number of dailies serving
Canadian cities affected the newspapers' ability to fulfill their responsibilities to the public. It was required to see how those circumstances
affected individuals, communities, and the country as a whole and to
make recommendations to remedy the problems it might discover.

The newspaper industry, which had successfully fended off the Press
Ownership Review Board, which the Davey Committee had strongly recommended in 1970, reacted with hostility to suggestions of any need for
government interference. Mild self-regulation in the form of voluntary
(and therefore not universal) press councils had been the only response
in the 1970s to public concerns about newspaper operations, and press
councils had no role at all in ownership questions. While newspapers
had lost their pre-eminence to television, they still remained, as both
the Davey Committee and Kent Commission demonstrated, highly profitable businesses for the most part. In their efforts to forestall any action
that would limit freedom to run their businesses as they saw fit, they
raised the spectre of government control and censorship. In so doing,

they again demonstrated the difficulty of assessing the proper balance between sometimes conflicting roles of newspapers as profit-seeking businesses and socially responsible information media.

The Kent Commission found that ownership in the industry, which was highly concentrated in 1970, was even more intensely so in 1980. In terms of circulation, the market held by English-language independent papers shrank from 39.6% to 25.7% during the ten year period. Among the French-language papers, the change was even more dramatic, with the independents' share of the market dwindling to 10% in 1980 from the 50.8% they had held in 1970. As a part of this trend, already large conglomerates had grown even larger. For example, Southam News increased its share of circulation from 21.5% in 1970 to 32.8% in 1980. The Thomson chain, by acquiring Free Press Publications, saw its circulation rise from 10.4% to 25.5%. In francophone Canada, Quebecor rose to predominance with 46.5% of circulation from its 11% base in 1970.[9]

While studies have shown that assumption of ownership by chains has led to some changes in news priorities and sources of information of individual papers, these changes cannot necessarily be interpreted as deleterious.[10] Moreover, other studies have failed to find evidence of chain direction of editorial opinion or efforts to either highlight or suppress particular issues in straight news reporting.[11] In research the present authors did for the Kent Commission regarding the impact of chain ownership in 1979 election coverage, no association between ownership and pattern of news reporting was found.[12] Nonetheless, the concentration of ownership had reached what many considered to be the level of a clear and present danger, when the elimination of competition in many cities left only one newspaper voice for readers. Also, it could be argued, the country-wide network of ownership provided the opportunity for controlling the direction of editorial policy. Further, newspaper chains are frequently only part of larger corporate conglomerates. These business empires may be more prone to view newspapers simply from the profit perspective, and thus consider the production of a quality product only a secondary consideration.

The Kent Commission concluded that the newspaper as a political institution was in less than good health. The Commission reported "a national consensus" regarding the decline of the newspaper as an instrument of political journalism, and linked this decline to a number of factors. Among these were: imitation of television's focus on the leadership dimension and the consequent failure to exercise the very strength of the newspaper, that is, "depth and comprehensiveness," and the concentration of newspaper ownership, leading to a withdrawal "from commitment on issues of national importance." In this regard, the Commission was also quick to point out that strong influence from a few corporate board rooms was equally unacceptable. Their solution to the problem was "to reinvigorate the national influence of independent editorial voices."[13]

These views on newspaper performance almost inevitably led to the kind of recommendations put forward by the Commission. In its proposed Canadian Newspaper Act, the Commission sought to forestall increased concentration and cross-ownership of media to remedy the most blatant current abuses of concentration of ownership, and, on the positive side, to encourage a wide base of newspaper ownership.[14]

Recommendations were also directed toward enhancing the independent role of journalists, and toward establishing a stronger voice for the community whose interests are affected by the quality of the newspaper. A press rights panel would be established "in conjunction with the Canadian Human Rights Commission. . .which would monitor the implementation and effectiveness of the legislation."[15] It recommended changes in the tax structure to encourage greater concern for "the provision of information." Finally, it suggested a subsidy for Canadian news services, so that domestic news would be improved and international news presented from a Canadian perspective.

The newspaper industry (although not all of those who worked for it) was no more pleased with the recommendations of the Kent Commission than they had been with its creation in the first place. It was predictable that a virtually unregulated industry would view even a mild form of regulation as unacceptable. Owners were quick to use the public's devotion to the concept of a free press, and its place in democracy, as the cornerstone of their arguments that they should be free to own as many newspapers as they could afford to buy. Canadian Press (CP) carved itself a niche in Canadian history by becoming one of the few organizations to tell the government that it didn't want its money.

Arthur Siegel has presented a thoughtful critique of the procedures as well as the recommendations of the Kent Commission. On balance, his assessment is not a favorable one. Among other things, Siegel points out as faults the haste with which the Commission reached its conclusions (one year as opposed to three years for a similar inquiry in Great Britain), the small size of the Commission (three members) given the scope of their concern, and that the commissioners may well have had preconceived notions, given their previous associations with media organizations. These problems, Siegel believes, perhaps preordained that the Report itself would have internal contradictions.

Siegel points to two contradictions between the Commission's findings and recommendations based on them. One deals with the perceptions of the Canadian public with the quality of Canadian newspapers. Here the Commission ignores its own survey research, which indicates a reasonably high regard for newspaper quality and substitutes its own impression, based on its hearings and letters to it, that the public is dissatisfied with the nation's press. Siegel characterizes this as an elitist attitude. The other contradiction deals with the differing attitudes that the Commission expressed regarding concentration of ownership in English-speaking Canada, as opposed to the even greater concentration of ownership in Quebec. Siegel dismisses as totally inadequate the Commission's justifications for being less upset by the chain domination of the French press.[16]

Newspaper Coverage of the 1979
Election Campaign

The data on Canadian newspaper coverage of the 1979 election in this chapter were gathered from twenty-three newspapers from across the country. These papers were selected to represent every province and both official languages. In addition, we sought to include newspapers owned by all the major chains as well as the prominent independents. The group of papers includes large, medium, and small circulation dailies. Papers with traditions of Liberal and Progressive Conservative support as well as those with no clear party ties were chosen. The two major metropolitan centres of Toronto and Montreal have multiple representation. Unfortunately a strike in Vancouver took the newspapers of that city out of circulation during the campaign. In sum, however, the sample of papers includes a very broad spectrum of the newspaper coverage available to Canadians across the country during the 1979 election campaign. These newspapers are as follows: the St. John's *Evening Telegram*, the Halifax *Chronicle-Herald*, the Charlottetown *Guardian*, the Saint John *Telegraph-Journal*, *Le Evangeline* (Moncton), *Le Soleil* (Quebec City), *La Tribune* (Sherbrooke), *Le Devoir* (Montreal), *La Presse* (Montreal), the Montreal *Star*, the Montreal *Gazette*, *Le Droit* (Ottawa), the Ottawa *Journal*, the Ottawa *Citizen*, the Toronto *Star*, the Toronto *Globe and Mail*, The Windsor *Star*, the Winnipeg *Free Press*, the Regina *Leader-Post*, the Edmonton *Journal*, the Calgary *Herald*, the Victoria *Daily Colonist*, and the suburban Vancouver paper, the *Columbian*, which we substituted for the Vancouver *Sun* and *Province*, both of which were on strike during the 1979 campaign.

In examining newspaper coverage there are some modifications in the way in which the data are presented. Since our newspaper sample stretches across the country, and since regionalism is one of the most salient features of the Canadian political scene, we will examine region as a possible determinant of coverage in conjunction with language analysis. Following this, we will deal with the organizational macrogate; in the case of newspapers this will focus on differences in coverage by chain and independent newspapers. We have grouped the organizational data into chain and independent papers, doing a separate analysis for each language group. This is done because in work for the Kent Commission we were unable to detect any significant influence of ownership on campaign reporting, and because the Commission in its own findings distinguished between the importance of concentration of ownership in anglophone Canada as opposed to francophone Canada. As in the case of the electronic media, we will examine issue and party agendas, as well as the evaluative material dealing with the major party leaders and parties. Data in the tables in this chapter are composed of all newspaper content studied; that is, front page stories, editorials, features, and cartoons. Earlier analysis revealed very strong correlations between all these types of content with the exception of cartoons.[17] Since these are so few in number, and in order to minimize the number of tables, all of these categories of content are grouped together.

Election Issue Coverage by Region
and Language

Table 4-1 presents the press issue agenda of the 1979 campaign, by region. Our initial observation is that the newspaper agenda is strikingly similar to those of radio and television discussed in the previous chapter. We are, in effect, dealing with a single mass media agenda in the 1979 election. Perhaps we should not be surprised, because all media were, after all, reporting on the same election. However, if the media alter information according to their own characteristics, one might have expected certain issues to be more attractive to a particular medium. No doubt, how the campaign issues were presented varied considerably between the electronic media and the newspaper, but what subjects were presented and in what order of importance were remarkably consistent. What variation did exist between the electronic and press agenda was at the lower end of the list of major issues, where stories concerning polls and administration of justice replaced economic development on the press agenda. As for the upper end of the scale, we note that stories on federal-provincial relations occupied a higher place for newspapers than they did for radio and television, while unemployment occupied a lower position on the newspaper rank order than it did on that of the electronic media.

When one looks at the regional variation in newspaper agendas, one is struck by the absence of major differences between regions. Leadership is the most important issue in every region, having greatest salience in Quebec and least in British Columbia. National unity was of most importance in the central provinces and less so elsewhere, perhaps mirroring the traditional conception of how this issue impacts on the public. This is true also of Quebec separatism, which peaks, naturally, in Quebec. Federal-provincial relations are more salient in Atlantic Canada and the prairies (although not in British Columbia) than they are in Quebec and Ontario. On economic issues, inflation was more widely mentioned in the prairies and British Columbia, where it occupied second place on both provincial agendas. Unemployment had a higher rank order in British Columbia and Atlantic Canada than it did in the prairies and the central provinces. Domestic gas and oil policy evoked more interest on the prairies, which included the producer provinces, and Atlantic Canada, which hoped to be producers, than it did in other regions dominated by consumer interests. The question of tax reform, which was most widely debated in the context of the mortgage plan proposed by the Progressive Conservatives, got amazingly consistent coverage in all regions. But returning to our initial theme, these variations are less impressive than the consistency with which the issues were accorded prominence in the various regions.

This consistency is apparent in the Spearman Rank-order Correlations shown in Table 4-2, where the lowest correlation is in fact very high, + .66, between the agendas of Atlantic Canada and B.C. The prairies and Atlantic Canada, and the prairies and Ontario have correla-

Table 4-1 — Percentage of Electoral Stories Dealing with Major Issues in the 1979 Campaign, by Region (with Rank Order)

REGION

CAMPAIGN ISSUE	ATLANTIC CANADA (N=1101) %	R/O	QUEBEC (N=1312) %	R/O	ONTARIO (N=1546) %	R/O	PRAIRIES (N=952) %	R/O	BRITISH COLUMBIA (N=276) %	R/O
Leadership	21.6	(1)	29.0	(1)	27.4	(1)	26.6	(1)	19.2	(1)
National Unity	17.5	(2)	23.6	(3)	20.6	(2)	18.1	(3)	12.0	(3)
Quebec Separatism	12.1	(7)	27.4	(2)	14.9	(3)	13.8	(5)	9.4	(5)
Inflation	17.2	(4)	11.4	(5)	11.7	(4)	18.4	(2)	18.8	(2)
Federal-Provincial Relations (non-separatism)	17.4	(3)	14.5	(4)	10.5	(5)	17.9	(4)	6.9	(8)
Unemployment	14.4	(5)	8.5	(6)	9.3	(6)	9.8	(7)	10.1	(4)
Domestic Gas & Oil Policy (Including Petro-Can)	12.2	(6)	5.0	(10)	8.8	(7)	13.7	(6)	5.8	(9)
Tax Reform (including Mortgage Interest Plans)	7.6	(8)	5.2	(8)	8.2	(8)	8.8	(8)	7.6	(7)
Polls	2.5	(11)	7.8	(7)	6.0	(11)	5.1	(10)	8.3	(6)
Administration of Justice	4.1	(10)	5.2	(8)	6.6	(9)	4.7	(11)	5.8	(9)
Television Debate	4.3	(9)	4.8	(11)	6.4	(10)	5.9	(9)	3.6	(11)

Table 4-2 — Spearman Rank-Order Correlation between Regional Agenda in the 1979 Campaign*

	QUEBEC	ONTARIO	PRAIRIES	BRITISH COLUMBIA
ATLANTIC CANADA	.72	.89	.93	.66
QUEBEC	—	.89	.74	.81
ONTARIO	—	—	.92	.76
PRAIRIES	—	—	—	.73

*all correlations are positive

tions of +.93 and +.92 respectively, which demonstrates a very high level of agreement regarding which major issues should be given most prominence.

The linguistic division in Canada is often portrayed as "two solitudes." It thus has suggested itself to us as one of the likely macro-gates in the gatekeeping process. However, it did not produce the degree of variation that one might have expected. As a matter of fact, agendas produced by French and English newspapers had a higher Spearman Rank-order Correlation, +.76, than was true of French and English electronic media.

Table 4-3 — Percentage of Electoral Stories Dealing with Major Issues in the 1979 Campaign, by Language (with Rank Order)

CAMPAIGN ISSUE	LANGUAGE			
	FRENCH (N = 1006)		ENGLISH (N = 4181)	
	%	R/O	%	R/O
Leadership	24.0	(1)	26.5	(1)
National Unity	18.3	3)	20.2	(2)
Quebec Separatism	22.6	(2)	15.6	(4)
Inflation	8.1	(6)	15.9	(3)
Federal-Provincial Relations (non-separatism)	11.0	(4)	14.9	(5)
Unemployment	8.3	(5)	10.8	(6)
Domestic Gas and Oil Policy (including Petro-Can)	3.1	(11)	10.8	(7)
Tax Reform (including Mortgage Interest Plans)	3.4	(10)	8.4	(8)
Polls	6.7	(7)	5.4	(10)
Administration of Justice	5.3	(8)	5.3	(11)
Television Debate	4.5	(9)	5.5	(9)

It might be argued that the reverse should be true, for after all, the CBC has a French and English service in both radio and television and they have a common senior management and legislative mandate. Newspaper chains, however, are either French or English in ownership, and have no legislative mandate, let alone a common one. Nonetheless, we see that although there are variations in the rank order and the percentage of stories on particular issues, the French and English agenda are in agreement about what is on the top half of their agenda, as opposed to what is on the bottom half. Leadership has pride of place in both languages. National unity has relatively the same importance in both languages. Quebec separatism, for obvious reasons, gets more attention and a higher rank order in French than in English, while the reverse is true for federal-provincial relations. This parallels the finding reported with regard to regions. The most pronounced difference is reflected in the differing coverage of inflation and domestic gas and oil policy, where English newspapers accorded these issues higher ranking and decidedly more coverage than did the French.

Party Coverage

Table 4-4 shows the distribution of stories dealing with the major parties involved in the 1979 campaign, by region. It is apparent that the governing party is accorded significantly greater attention in the press. The smallest gap between the Liberals and the Progressive Conservatives occurs in Ontario, and even there it was 12.4%. In Quebec this difference was a full 27.2%. The Progressive Conservative Party was second in all regions, ahead of the New Democratic Party by a margin almost identical to that by which it trailed the Liberals. The New Democrats got their highest percentage of story mentions in British Columbia, but even here trailed the PCs by 11.6%. In Quebec and Atlantic Canada the NDP bottomed out in coverage, reflecting their inability to make a significant electoral impact east of Ontario. In Quebec, the Social Credit Party, which had been a significant contestant for seats in the previous two decades, and the Parti Québecois, whose control of the Quebec government and active role in the sovereignty-association referendum made it a potentially important actor in the federal election, received noteworthy attention. This was not the case in other regions.

The increasingly extreme differences in vote-getting capabilities of the two major political parties across Canada is not reflected in this table. Most obviously the Liberals do well in attracting coverage in areas where they fail abysmally in winning seats. The Progressive Conservatives, on the other hand, received only slightly fewer mentions in Quebec, where they do poorly, than they did in British Columbia, which is relatively good electoral territory for them. It seems that gatekeeping decisions by newspapers in the various regions of the country are dictated by the national prominence of political parties, with only modest variations being fostered by the regional strength of a party.

Table 4-4 — Percentage of Electoral Stories Dealing with
Major Parties in the 1979 Campaign, by Region

			REGION		
PARTY	ATLANTIC CANADA (N=1101)	QUEBEC (N=1312)	ONTARIO (N=1546)	PRAIRIES (N=952)	BRITISH COLUMBIA (N=276)
Liberal	55.3	67.6	62.6	61.7	60.9
Progressive Conservative	37.4	40.4	50.2	46.0	42.8
New Democratic Party	23.3	22.0	29.5	27.6	31.2
Social Credit/Raillement Créditiste	3.3	14.5	8.2	5.4	5.4
Parti Québecois	5.4	22.0	8.8	6.9	3.6

Table 4-5 — Percentage of Electoral Stories Dealing with
           Major Parties in the 1979 Campaign, by Language

| | LANGUAGE | |
| | FRENCH | ENGLISH |
PARTY	(N = 1006)	(N = 4181)
Liberal	72.7	59.5
Progressive Conservative	42.7	44.1
New Democratic Party	24.0	26.5
Social Credit/Raillement Créditiste	19.0	5.5
Parti Québecois	19.0	8.8

Table 4-5 deals with the impact of language on gatekeeping decisions.
Here we find that language, for the most part, follows regional considerations. Thus one finds that the major differences between the language
groups have to do with Social Credit and the Parti Québecois, both of
which are of course, Quebec-based parties. The same rank order relationship exists among the three major parties, with the Liberals having greater
salience in the French press. Despite their lack of electoral success in
areas served by the French press, both the Progressive Conservative Party
and the New Democratic Party received only slightly less attention in
the French press than in the English. As with region, language did not
in any dramatic way alter the extent of coverage of political parties.

Evaluation of Party Leaders and Parties

As with the electronic media, newspapers found it difficult to avoid fram-
ing news items in a manner that might convey a positive or negative
impression of electoral participants. Table 4-6 reflects not only news
stories, but also editorials, features, and cartoons where this kind of impact is consciously sought.

It is surprising that newspapers do not contain far more evaluative
material than we found in radio and television newscasts. Only in the
newspapers of the prairies and British Columbia, with respect to treatment of the Liberal Party, do we see a decided tendency toward negative
evaluation at a level much higher than found on radio and television.
This may give us cause to reflect that television and radio are more critical media, despite their lack of editorial traditions, possibly because they
seek out the confrontational aspects of party strategies. That is, they are
more prone to carry the film clip in which one party leader attacks the
other leader and his party, rather than being inclined to feature those
parts of speeches devoted to the explanation of party policy. Politicians
have reacted to this propensity by structuring their remarks to feed this
appetite.

Another similarity between the press and the electronic media is the
propensity toward more negative than positive evaluation, especially

Table 4-6 — Percentage of Electoral Stories Reflecting Positively and Negatively on Major Party Leaders and Parties in the 1979 Campaign, by Region

REGION

	ATLANTIC CANADA (N=1101)		QUEBEC (N=1312)		ONTARIO (N=1546)		PRAIRIES (N=952)		BRITISH COLUMBIA (N=276)	
	POS.	NEG.	POS.	NEG.	POS.	NEG.	POS.	NEG.	POS.	NEG.
Trudeau	1.5	7.1	2.7	6.6	2.6	8.5	1.7	8.9	1.8	10.9
Clark	1.2	4.1	1.6	6.1	1.6	9.3	2.5	6.5	1.8	3.3
Broadbent	0.7	0.6	1.2	0.6	1.6	0.9	1.8	0.8	0	0.7
Liberal	4.6	17.3	4.4	14.8	4.8	16.6	4.8	23.9	1.4	26.6
PC	5.0	5.5	4.5	6.6	3.3	10.6	7.3	8.7	7.6	6.2
NDP	2.3	1.3	1.7	1.4	2.6	1.5	3.0	1.8	1.4	3.7

for the two major parties, and of these, most dramatically for the Liberals. For instance, British Columbia newspapers implied criticism in 26.6% of their stories dealing with the Liberal Party, but only in 1.4% could one derive a positive image of the party. These figures are only marginally less impressive in prairie newspapers. What is perhaps more surprising is that Quebec newspapers, while presenting the Liberals in a somewhat less critical vein, still were decidedly more critical than approving. The Progressive Conservatives were treated more kindly overall, with only Ontario newspapers displaying the kind of intense negative portrayal that had been characteristic of treatment of the Liberals. The New Democratic Party, while not the subject of much evaluative commentary at all, had a slightly positive treatment everywhere but in British Columbia. It seems, therefore, that a combination of the tendency of media to report the negative things that one party says about another, together with their critical attitudes toward the governing party, led to a negative evaluation of the Liberal Party in all regions, but most especially in western Canada. The Progressive Conservative Party was also evaluated negatively nearly everywhere, most especially in Ontario.

These findings are mirrored in the treatment of the three party leaders as well. Once again, we find that the newspapers were not as prone toward negativism as were the electronic media but did have the same comparative ordering of their treatment of Trudeau, Clark, and Broadbent, with the Liberal leader receiving the greatest amount of negative commentary. Again, this was most prominent in western newspapers, and least prominent in Quebec. Mr. Clark was treated more negatively than was his party and this reflects the conventional wisdom that surrounded his performance as a party leader. In the crucial province of Ontario, he received even more negative commentary than did Mr. Trudeau, and not even in British Columbia did positive comments outweigh the negative ones. The evaluative treatment of Mr. Broadbent was slight, and relatively balanced in all regions. Thus across all regions of the country newspapers accorded the two major party leaders negative treatment. If

Table 4-7 — Percentage of Electoral Stories Reflecting Positively and Negatively on Major Party Leaders and Parties in the 1979 Campaign, by Language

	LANGUAGE			
	FRENCH (N = 1006)		ENGLISH (N = 4181)	
	POS.	NEG.	POS.	NEG.
Trudeau	2.4	4.1	2.1	8.8
Clark	0.5	5.5	2.0	6.8
Broadbent	0.8	0.3	1.4	0.9
Liberal	3.8	9.4	4.6	20.2
PC	1.9	6.0	5.5	8.3
NDP	1.5	0.9	2.5	1.6

either was supposed to lend a charismatic presence to the campaign, it wasn't reflected in the pages of the nation's press.

When one looks at language as a factor influencing the evaluative direction of newspaper material dealing with parties and party leaders, one finds the same negative direction both in French and English newspapers. There is a tendency for the English press to be more negative toward the Liberal Party and its leader than is the case for the French press. Aside from that, language seems not to be a decisive basis for predicting how particular parties or leaders will be presented by the print media. The English press, however, does appear to be more inclined to evaluative reporting of one kind or another than its French counterpart.

Chain Ownership and Electoral Coverage

The question of chain ownership was at the heart of the Kent Commission deliberations. The problems inherent in this pattern of ownership were considered to be major by the Commission, although somewhat less so among the French chains than English, despite the fact that concentration of ownership is higher among Quebec newspapers.[18] As mentioned earlier in this chapter, Arthur Siegel argues that this conclusion is not satisfactorily explained in the Report. Tables 4-8 and 4-9 were constructed to shed some light on this debate.

We can see from Table 4-8 that the rank ordering of percentages of stories devoted to the political parties and major electoral issues are quite consistent from chain-owned to independent papers within each language group. On the French side, two items appear "out of step" between independent and chain papers. These are the percentages of stories dealing with the Progressive Conservative Party, which is notably higher among independent papers, and the Quebec separatism issue, which is similarly higher in the chain-owned papers. No other issue or party seemed to generate differential interest of more than five to six percent, and most were close to even. On the English side, there is even less variation between chain and independent papers, with unemployment being the only issue on which the difference in coverage was over 7%. Independent papers touched on this issue more frequently than did chain-owned ones. Thus, as was the case with our earlier analyses, we do not perceive that chain ownership had an evident effect on campaign reporting as far as issue emphasis is concerned.

On the question of the evaluative dimension in news presentation, both reportorial and interpretive, we do see some differences between chain-owned and independent papers in the two language groups. The independent newspapers in the French language were more negative in their evaluation of both major parties and their leaders than was the case with their chain-owned counterparts. While the differences are not striking, they are nonetheless consistent. An examination of the English language chain-owned and independent papers, moreover, reveals a consistent pattern of greater negativism for the two major parties and their

Table 4-8 — Percentage of Electoral Stories Dealing with
Major Parties and Issues in the 1979 Campaign,
by Chain and Independent Ownership,
Controlling for Language

| | LANGUAGE | | | |
| | FRENCH | | ENGLISH | |
	INDEP (N = 470)	CHAIN (N = 536)	INDEP (N = 655)	CHAIN (N = 3526)
Liberal	73.8	71.6	54.5	60.4
PC	47.2	38.8	40.9	44.7
NDP	25.3	22.8	26.3	26.6
Leadership	21.5	26.1	22.0	27.3
National Unity	19.8	17.0	21.4	19.9
Quebec Separatism	17.4	27.1	14.7	15.8
Inflation	5.1	10.6	19.8	15.2
Federal-Provincial Relations (non-separatism)	12.1	10.1	20.5	13.8
Unemployment	7.4	9.0	17.1	9.7
Domestic Gas & Oil Policy (including Petro-Can)	3.6	2.6	14.7	10.1
Tax Reform (including Mortage Interest Plans)	2.3	4.3	9.9	8.1
Polls	3.4	9.5	3.8	5.7
Administration of Justice	5.3	5.2	5.5	5.3
Television Debate	4.5	4.5	3.8	5.8

leaders, this time among the chain-owned papers. This may in fact reflect to some degree the regional distribution of the chain-owned and
independent papers in our sample, as the bulk of western papers were
chain owned. While this, however, might explain the negativism toward
the Liberals and Trudeau, it does not account for that phenomenon with
respect to the Progressive Conservatives and Clark.

There is no ready explanation for the finding that it is the independents that are more negative in the French language and the chains that
are more negative in English. Nor can we say that one is necessarily
preferable to the other. Thus there is no corroboration here for the Kent
Commission conclusion that chains somehow constitute a greater threat
in English Canada than in French.

Conclusions

Contrary to our expectations, press treatment of the 1979 election campaign does not appear to have varied significantly on regional, linguistic,

Table 4-9 — Percentage of Electoral Stories Reflecting Positively or Negatively on Major Party Leaders and Parties in the 1979 Campaign, by Chain and Independent Ownership, Controlling for Language

	LANGUAGE							
	FRENCH				ENGLISH			
	INDEP (N=470)		CHAIN (N=536)		INDEP (N=655)		CHAIN (N=3526)	
	POS.	NEG.	POS.	NEG.	POS.	NEG.	POS.	NEG.
Trudeau	2.8	4.9	2.1	3.4	1.4	5.5	2.3	9.5
Clark	0.2	6.2	0.7	4.9	0.8	5.0	2.2	7.1
Broadbent	1.3	0.2	0.4	0.4	0.9	1.1	1.5	0.8
Liberal	4.7	11.2	2.8	7.8	6.7	16.3	4.2	21.0
PC	1.3	7.0	2.2	5.0	6.3	7.9	5.3	8.4
NDP	1.7	1.5	1.3	0.4	4.0	1.8	2.3	1.8

or ownership dimensions. In the previous chapter, dealing with radio and television, we reported finding a common electronic media agenda in 1979 campaign coverage, albeit with a French-language variation. Put in a different way, the macro-gates of media type, organization, and language did not appear to be functioning so as to filter, in any substantive way, the amount or type of information reaching the public. Partly because we were dealing in the case of radio and television with organizations that were, for the most part, national in scope, we might surmise that this phenomenon might account for the slight variations detected. When the press was brought into the analysis, permitting a comparative overview of media types, we expected to find some support for McLuhan's contention that content is likely to be modified by the medium through which it moves. While our data of course do not disprove that contention, neither do they support the idea that the "medium is the message." What is clear is that in the context of this particular election, similar agenda were produced by all three types of media studied.

Similarly, we had expected that regional variations within the print media would be far greater than we have found evidence for. We can only conclude that with respect to the 1979 election, at least, there was far more of a single national agenda which cut across all regions of the country, both languages, and all mass media, than we would have expected.

The important questions now are: how does one explain these findings, and what do they mean in terms of information flows in Canadian society? On this last question, we must point out that a national election may not be the most appropriate event on which to focus in order to reach valid conclusions about media behavior in general. Such an election is by definition a "national event," which forces media to highlight national issues as these are defined by political spokesmen and, perhaps, by other media outlets. On the other hand, while this might be understandable with respect to radio and television because of their basically national scope and comparative lack of opportunity for direct editorial commentary, it is less so with respect to newspapers, which in this country serve essentially local markets. The latter could choose to emphasize issues of local importance and to downplay or ignore others, especially in editorials and features, to a much greater extent than is apparently the case in the 1979 election. They could also choose to emphasize what politicians do not talk about more easily than would be possible for their electronic counterparts. That neither of these things happened to any recognizable extent is something for which we have no simple explanation.

We may speculate that some of the leading newspapers in the larger cities might exert an influence on their colleagues elsewhere, especially because of the existence of wire services, which might pick up their stories and disseminate them widely. Furthermore, the pack journalism phenonemon, which is a characteristic of the press gallery in ordinary times, is intensified by the structure of campaign coverage, where reporters follow leaders around the country for weeks on end. This atmosphere, and the influence of their electronic media colleagues, would no doubt incline them to horserace journalism. It is fair to say that the

common circumstances of those who reported the election played some
role in the similarity of the coverage they produced.

We are obviously not in a position to assert that the macro-gates that
we have identified have no impact on the information reaching the public.
While we now suspect that this impact may be considerably less and/or
more difficult to detect than has been commonly assumed, we recognize that further studies involving non-election contexts and perhaps a
more detailed examination of media characteristics will be necessary in
order to allow even a tentative suggestion of this kind.

Nonetheless, it should be emphasized that elections are important instruments of the national decision-making process, and that an investigation of the role of media in this process is therefore valuable. This is
especially true in a country such as Canada with its huge territory and
clearly identifiable regional and linguistic communities. A situation
where information passes in relatively undifferentiated form through
macro-gates such as we have described could prove to be of major importance in providing support for the national political community.

Notes

[1]*Royal Commission on Newspapers* (Ottawa: Minister of Supply and Services
Canada, 1981), p. 74.

[2]Among the most influential literature that stresses the dangers of chain
ownership are John Porter, *The Vertical Mosaic: An Analysis of Social Class
and Power in Canada* (Toronto: University of Toronto Press, 1965),
pp. 462-90; *Report of the Senate Committee on Mass Media, Vol. I, The
Uncertain Mirror* (Ottawa: The Queens Printer, 1970); and Wallace Clement,
The Canadian Corporate Elite: An Analysis of Economic Power (Toronto:
McClelland and Stewart, 1975), pp. 270, 324. The Kent Commission
considered the question of cross-media ownership and made a specific
recommendation to prevent it; see *Royal Commission on Newspapers*,
pp. 13-5, 227. This recommendation was acted on in an Order in Council of
July 29, 1982. It directed the CRTC to deny licences to broadcasters already
owning newspapers within a particular market area, as well as to oppose
renewals of licences under such conditions. See "Direction to the CRTC on
Issue and Renewal of Broadcast Licences to Daily Newspaper Proprietors,"
Canada Gazette Part II, Vol. 116, No. 15, pp. 2713-4.

[3]David Halberstam, *The Powers That Be* (New York: Dell Publishing, 1980),
p. 568.

[4]Ibid., pp. 538-47.

[5]See for example William O. Gilsdorf, "Getting the Message Across: The
Communication Strategy of the Federal Liberal Party in the 1979 and 1980
Canadian Federal Elections," paper presented to the Annual Meeting of the
Canadian Communication Association, Université de Québec à Montréal,
1980, pp. 33-4 and Clive Cocking, *Following the Leaders: A Media Watcher's
Diary of Campaign '79* (Toronto: Doubleday Canada, 1980), pp. 177-9;
278-88.

[6]On this point see Frederick J. Fletcher, *The Newspaper and Public Affairs*, Vol. 7. Research Publications, Royal Commission on Newspapers (Ottawa: Minister of Supply and Services Canada, 1981), p. 20, and Gilsdorf, pp. 34-5.

[7]Fletcher, p. 105.

[8]Watergate is the primary example of this type of newspaper reporting. For an account of the Washington *Post's* reporting strategy, see Halberstam, pp. 845-80.

[9]*Royal Commission on Newspapers*, pp. 2-3.

[10]W. I. Romanow and W. C. Soderlund, "The Southam Press Acquisition of The Windsor *Star*: A Canadian Case Study of Change," *Gazette: International Journal for Mass Communication Studies*, XXIV (1978), pp. 255-70.

[11]R. H. Wagenberg and W. C. Soderlund, "The Influence of Chain-Ownership on Editorial Comment in Canada," *Journalism Quarterly* 52 (Spring 1974), pp. 93-8; and "The Effects of Chain Ownership on Editorial Coverage: The Case of the 1974 Canadian Federal Election," *Canadian Journal of Political Science*, IX (December 1976), pp. 682-9.

[12]W. I. Romanow, W. C. Soderlund, R. H. Wagenberg, and E. D. Briggs, "Correlates of Newspaper Coverage of the 1979 Canadian Election: Chain-Ownership, Competitiveness of Market, and Circulation," Appendix III to Fletcher, *The Newspaper and Public Affairs*.

[13]*Royal Commission on Newspapers*, pp. 135-6.

[14]Ibid., p. 237.

[15]Ibid., p. 238.

[16]Arthur Siegel, *Politics and the Media in Canada* (Toronto: McGraw-Hill Ryerson, 1983), pp. 146-50.

[17]W. C. Soderlund, W. I. Romanow, E. D. Briggs, and R. H. Wagenberg, "Newspaper Coverage of the 1979 Canadian Federal Election: The Impact of Region, Language, and Chain-Ownership," paper presented at the annual meeting of the Canadian Communication Association, Dalhousie University, 1981.

[18]*Royal Commission on Newspapers*, pp. 114-6; 229.

5

The Other Side of the Coin: Government Regulation of Media

Implicit in democratic theory is the notion that citizens have access to information that allows them to judge the performance of governments. The few weeks of an election campaign serve to harden those judgments, and focus them into the major democratic decision as to who will rule. We have discussed in previous chapters the performance of the media in providing a basis for public judgments during elections, and the eagerness of political parties to utilize the media for partisan purposes. It has to be remembered that the media operate within a framework of rules and regulations that, apart from a few that are self-imposed, are created by the same governments about which they supposedly supply objective information to the public.

One of the forms of regulation applies directly to media behavior during elections. However, governments are also concerned with regulating media at other times and for other purposes than purely electoral ones. It is important, then, to examine the larger regulatory context within which media function. Central to this context is the demand that Canadian society has been making for a strengthened social, economic and political fibre so as to permit uniquely Canadian decisions about the destiny of Canadian society. This chapter will begin, therefore, with a general review of the principles and concerns that have influenced government-media relations over the years, proceed with an outline of successive regulatory instruments, and conclude with a discussion of the manner of regulating media during electoral campaigns.

The political system a state embraces profoundly affects the relationship between government and the communication system.[1]

In authoritarian systems, for instance, the media have little choice but to support the status quo, including those who hold the reins of power; media behavior is uncomplicated, the range of information is narrow, and the content stringently controlled. Media function not as independent systems, but only as extensions and instruments of the official state structure. Freedom of expression is not among the privileges accorded the media. In totalitarian societies based on rigid ideologies the media function is even more firmly directed in the interests of fostering the official belief system. It is not enough merely to prevent media challenges to the government, the media must play a central role in state propaganda and indoctrination programs. This function is characterized by state ownership of the media and total dictation of their messages, along with rigid control of public access to foreign communications.

Democratic and pluralistic societies, in contrast, have always encouraged the free development of communication systems. Indeed, democracies are today frequently identified and measured by the extent to which they exhibit a free press. The individual is best served, according to democratic ideals, when allowed to choose from many versions of the truth served up by multiple communications media, unfettered by government censorship.

Whatever the contrast between authoritarian/totalitarian and democratic societies, however, media performance at the best of times remains only a rough approximation of the democratic ideal. Media organizations and systems operate as business enterprises rather than as pure public service agencies, which means that profit must be a prime objective; that sources of financial well-being, as in the early days of press development, must be respected and courted; and that questions can consequently be raised concerning the purity of the information transmitted.[2]

Because of economic developments associated with mass media growth in the twentieth century, Western societies have come to question how well their media have been performing as open and free marketplaces of ideas. The rapid rise and sophistication of the advertising and public relations industries in particular have given impetus to such questioning. As media have cast themselves into social surveillance roles, and while they have assumed postures as defenders of freedom of expression, they have also serviced the economic system to such an extent that they are characterized by near-total dependency upon advertising. While this dual role is quite acceptable, say critics of mass media, they question which role, the socio-political or the economic, has become dominant in the media's day-to-day functioning.

Some contemporary attitudes about the societal role of media have coalesced under a theoretical framework that has been labelled *social responsibility*. This school of thought concentrates on what constitutes responsible media behavior within a highly competitive social advertising context. Such concerns found expression in reports of formal studies in the United States and the United Kingdom in the 1940s and 1950s, and more recently in Canada. We have in social responsibility theory a modern critical response to mass media behavior that found its genesis in the post–World War II phenomenon of Consumerism.[3]

There are several dominant characteristics of Consumerism as it relates to the mass media. Consumers have become better educated and more discriminating. Consumer groups have found that the mass media and politicians alike respond favorably to public demands for improved products and product safety. As a result, the federal Department of Consumer and Corporate Affairs was established; one of its functions is to monitor advertising activities.

Social responsibility theory affirms that it is essential that someone, even if it be government, ensure that media behave responsibly in their relationships with their societies. For example, press councils, established in 1970 in Canada, may be viewed as a response by media — although in this case urged by governments — to consumer demands. Press Councils often invite consumers to comment on corrective measures after they have ruled that media behavior has been improper. They also solicit consumer complaints about advertisements that are perceived to be fraudulent or misleading. Thus the private sector has provided access to an informal regulatory process. But in the public sector, the government has provided a legislatively formal input for consumers by holding public hearings for broadcasting licences. Such informal and formal processes have given consumer advocates an instrument to make mass media weigh their responsibilities carefully. Consumerism therefore encourages the type of self-regulatory and self-corrective initiatives that are assumed in the free marketplace model of media behavior. Where corrective measures do not occur as a consequence of media initiatives, social responsibility theory calls for government intervention to ensure that the public interest prevails.

Critical appraisals of media performance are useful to prompt continued vigilance against erosion of fundamental values and institutions. Governments in Canada, by and large, have been conscious of their role in this regard, but also of the dangers of the two extremes of the spectrum of intervention. Too much governmental direction and supervision of the media will not make them freer, but merely subject to a single voice — that of the government. On the other hand, complete non-intervention may mean that the broadly accepted goals of society are not adequately served. To achieve proper balance requires considerable skill and, as we will see, constant review.

The Canadian Experience

Two major political themes impose themselves on the public policy discussion relating to the media: the need to protect Canada from cultural domination by the United States, and the need to promote national political and social consciousness in a country that has strong regional identities.

The role of the media in fostering a national consciousness has been a vital concern for Canadians. Successive governments have cast inquiring eyes at the operation of the Canadian communication system and have sought to define and perfect it for national purposes. This indicates an implicit acceptance of Karl Deutsch's theory, which we discussed in Chapter 2, that a strong relationship exists between the area covered by a communication system and the boundaries of a state. It is thus appropriate to delve more deeply into governments' self-conscious examination of media systems within their political realms.

Political integration is a much-sought-after goal for the leaders of central governments in states such as Canada, which have strong regional traditions. Nation-building is the term used to describe the variety of policies undertaken by governments to achieve this end. In Canada in 1871, for instance, a National Policy revolving around tariffs was put forward to weld an identifiable national economy. Canada was created, however, out of a series of regional identities and nation-building has always had to contend with province-building.[4] Wielders of power at the national level have had to work to create a definition of a Pan-Canadian society and provide a focus for the expression of the aspirations of that society. The term *national unity* in Canada serves to summarize this goal.

The media as transmitters of ideas have a crucial role to play in this process. From the time electronic media became popular (radio in the 1920s and television in the 1950s), the federal government took steps to control their development so that they could be marshalled to perform their designated tasks in nation-building. This control sought to buttress the political boundaries of Canada with a communication system that would prevent American penetration from becoming overwhelming, while at the same time moderating the parochial effects of provincial identities on national consciousness. Neither the United States nor the provinces have ceased to present a challenge to the nation-building role of Canadian media and thus the debate over the proper function of the Canadian communication system has continued unabated.

In the last decades of the twentieth century, Canadian governments are caught up in the complex problem of determining how the media can play a useful role in helping society to achieve broadly accepted goals. The complications are multiplied when consensus on goals is not readily apparent. But democratic societies have purposes, which include the fostering of free speech, and in this regard the roles of the communication systems are vital. With these standards in mind, the Canadian government over the years has had to construct laws governing communications that have had to balance the rights of society as opposed to individuals, public versus private ownership, content regulation as distinct from non-interference, and other often conflicting claims on policy. Out of these decades of debate there has emerged a system of mixed public and private ownership of electronic media governed by the same set of rules, while the print media have remained privately owned and almost untouched by legislation, other than that which regulates most businesses.

Governments have concerns about mass media that are not related to the demands of nation-building. Even in those societies where there is general agreement that a large measure of media freedom exists, there are obligatory regulatory functions to be performed. For example, the media function in Western societies as business organizations, so business licences are required. As well, regulations exist regarding the use of government mail systems by print media. Income taxes, duties, and excise taxes are all regulatory factors to be considered when reviewing frameworks within which media function.

In the electronic media of radio, television, and cable television, the regulatory role of government is most pronounced. There are several reasons for such a heavy involvement by government. First, there would be technical chaos without, at a minimum, an agreement to allocate broadcasting frequencies, both between and within countries. Second, until recent technological advances brought about changes in the broadcasting spectrum, frequencies were considered to be scarce resources and it was important that a selection process within each country be instituted to determine who would be granted or denied the use of these resources. Third, because they might be subject to misuse or abuse, licences were awarded to broadcasters for only a specified period of time. By forcing a licencee to reapply for permission to continue using the allocated frequency, governments exercise some control over media behavior. In some states, this minimal degree of regulation has grown to include all facets of broadcasting up to and including the censorship of content.

The question of the appropriate amount of government involvement in media operations is both perpetual and complex. It involves not only regulation but also the ownership of media organizations. In the United Kingdom, for example, the British Broadcasting Company was established in 1922 and was privately owned by radio equipment manufacturers. Five years later, given concerns about the power which this new medium was considered to wield over public opinion, the private company was dissolved, the member owners were reimbursed for their interests, and the resources were assumed by an independent Crown corporation, the British Broadcasting Corporation.[5] In the late 1950s public pressure and demands for more popular entertainment formats forced Parliament in the United Kingdom to grant broadcast programming licences (for radio and television) to private owners, who operate in a less restricted, but still regulated, environment. Even then, the hardware distribution systems, the broadcasting stations and transmitters continue to be owned by the Crown.

On the other hand, private ownership of media has always characterized the media systems of the United States. While some recent developments in Public Broadcasting Systems (PBS) have been markedly successful, ownership of such organizations is retained by co-operative associations or by colleges and universities, rather than by formal government structures. Given American traditions, the development of government-owned media systems is unlikely.

As in many other areas of public policy the influence of the British and American models has had an impact on Canadian thinking and often led to decisions that incorporated elements from both countries. Media systems in Canadian society have, from the early 1920s, been subjected to a variety of social and political pressures to function completely as private enterprise organizations, or completely as publicly owned organizations, operating as Crown corporations. Despite (or perhaps because of) these contending forces, Canada has tended to settle somewhere in between the two positions, in what appears to be a compatible mix of the two forms of ownership.

The debate continues, however, and the merits of both forms continue to be espoused in Canadian society. Those who prefer collective ownership point to its successes in public utilities. Collective ownership or management has always been with us, they insist, and point to police forces, fire-fighting forces, and power and hydro organizations as examples of how the common good can benefit from public management or ownership. On the other hand, those who extol the benefits of private individual ownership counter with arguments about the dangers of excessive governmental-bureaucratic control. Further, they add, information is not the sort of public commodity that can be pushed in measured amounts through a public utility pipe. While the debate goes on, and is likely to continue, it is clear that the government regulatory role in Canada continues to expand. In that expansion, concerns about harnessing all media in nation-building continue to be expressed.

As was pointed out earlier, government regulation over electronic media is a natural consequence of the characteristics of broadcasting. This same control over other media is not as natural or pervasive. Nonetheless, with increasing concern about national political and cultural identities, which are threatened by a rapid development—a virtual explosion—of media content-distribution systems, governments in Western societies are looking to all informational media to adopt social consciousness roles.

A National Political, Social, and Cultural Identity

In pursuit of a national identity, Canada has consciously assigned a defensive role to its communication system. Indeed, Canada's concerns go considerably beyond pure political concerns—Canada's culture is at stake, concludes the latest of many Royal Commissions or committees charged with reviewing the role of media in the Canadian social structure.[6]

The history of Canadian media is heavily punctuated by study after study— of a formal or informal nature—focusing on the threat emanating from the massive onslaught of American information. These studies invariably have concluded that Canadian media should play a prominent role in defending Canada's identity, and that the federal government should be instrumental in harnessing the nation's media resources to fulfil that defensive function. There are some Canadians who, crying "censorship," oppose any extension of government control over what Canadians may see and hear. Others, such as Harry Boyle, have argued that the dominance of one state over another, even if unplanned, stifles a society's self-expression, and could be the "most vulgar censorship of all."[7]

National goals may lack clear political definition and, indeed, may vary in definition considerably from region to region, as they do in Canada. In large part, however, broad agreement is likely to be found on one central issue: Canadians have a strong preference to be recognized as members of a separate, distinct political entity rather than to be regarded, broadly, as "Americans."

The growing phenomenon of Canadian nationalism concerning media affairs is the key issue here. To understand the nature and intent of the strategies adopted by Canadian regulatory agencies, one must appreciate the developing nationalism that motivates policy-makers as they pursue the elusive goal of national integration.

Nationalist goals are further frustrated by Canada's heavy dependence on the United States as an export market and as a source of imports. American economic influence reaches most directly into the domestic economy in terms of direct investment (hence ownership and control) in the industrial and resource sectors. One writer on Canada's financial affairs was moved to comment that "In the 3½ decades after World War II, Canada gained a dubious renown as the world's most prosperous satellite economy."[8]

There is clear evidence that the strong US hold over the Canadian economy has been recently lessened. For example, the net inflow of US direct investment in all industries fell from a 1965-75 annual average of $551 million to a 1976-79 average of $36 million.[9] To what extent such trends will continue is speculative at this point. Nevertheless, the historical pattern of US dominance has given substance to characterizations of Canada as having a branch plant economy and its people having a colonial mentality. And, some would argue, such historical control has determined the broad outline of Canadian cultural activities.[10]

However, even without the strong economic ties that cause cultural information to flow from the United States to Canada, there has always been a strong preference by Canadians for mass media content from the United States.[11] Thus from almost the beginning of broadcasting, Canadian regulations were framed with an eye to forestalling wholesale American penetration. Canadian content regulations enacted for television in 1959-60 were clearly designed to encourage an east-west flow of information within Canada as a counter to the south-to-north flow from the United States.

More than thirty years earlier, the first Royal Commission on Broadcasting affairs, the Aird Commission (named after its chairman, Sir John Aird) had stressed that the destiny of Canada depended upon the ability and willingness of Canadians to "control and utilize our own internal communications for Canadian purposes."[12] The note struck by the Aird Report, about the need for Canadians to control their destiny, became the first in a lengthy series of comments that have emphasized that Canada should have a broadcasting system that is uniquely Canadian.

A more recent and more comprehensive insistence along these lines — more comprehensive in that it considered and anticipated the broader impact of telecommunications systems — was contained in a Green Paper tabled in the House of Commons in 1973 by the federal Minister of Communications, Gerard Pelletier.[13] It stressed that the continuing obligation to mobilize Canadian creative, production, and distribution resources is in the interests of the nation, but also emphasized that this was not a responsibility for the federal government alone, but is an urgent concern for all governments, the communications industry, and the general public. It added that the rapid technological developments envisioned for the immediate future raised serious problems concerning the free flow of information:

> These are of specifically urgent concern for Canada because of its proximity to the United States, where the generation of information and entertainment is on a scale that threatens to overwhelm Canadian cultural resources, creative capacity, and sources of information and to constrict the means of access to them. It is therefore essential that a high priority be given to the accelerated development of Canadian creative resources, and to greatly increased production and distribution facilities.[14]

Thus a consistency of obligation for Canadian media stretches from the Aird Report of 1929, through the Green Paper of 1973, right up to the 1982 Report of the Federal Cultural Policy Review Committee (the Applebaum-Hébert Report): media must protect Canadian society from domination by information from the United States. Other inquiries over the years have also stressed that basic message, and shed further light on the mass media regulatory system in Canada.

Canada's broadcasting systems have been regulated by four Broadcasting Acts, enacted in 1932, 1936, 1958, and 1968. These Acts adopted after extensive public debate, demonstrate how the direction for Canada's broadcasting systems has been progressively moulded and defined. There has been a consistency to the investigations and public discussions that resulted in the successive Broadcasting Acts: Canada, if it is to be a clearly identifiable political entity, has specific urgent needs, and Canada's mass media can contribute to the attainment of goals that will satisfy those needs.

A review of events leading up to the enactment of each of the four Acts, and of the events surrounding the Acts, will identify particular regulatory bodies and their strategies in fulfilling national goals.

1932 Broadcasting Act:
First Comprehensive Regulation

Prior to the first of the broadcast Acts, broadcasting and radiotelegraphy were subject to the authority of the Wireless Telegraph Act of 1905, the Telegraphs Act of 1906, and the Radiotelegraph Act of 1913. It was under the authority of the last Act, in 1922, that it was stipulated that only British subjects could receive transmitting licences.[15] At the time, radio transmitter licences were owned, by and large, by newspapers and by companies whose prime concern was the manufacturing and marketing of electrical supplies (Bell Telephone, Marconi, and Westinghouse, for example).[16]

While these stations were assigned to private owners or companies, concurrent with their development was the decision in 1923 by Sir Henry

Thornton, president of the Canadian National Railways (by then a nationalized rail system) to furnish radio entertainment to passengers on that system's rail service. Thornton's biographer has noted that as a result of his ability to recognize the inherent possibilities in the new medium, the concept of public broadcasting became emphasized:

> Thornton saw radio as a great unifying force in Canada; to him the political conception transcended the commercial, and he set out consciously to create a sense of nationhood through the medium of the Canadian National Railway service.[17]

National transportation systems were viewed at the time as an essential east-west axis to offer a sense of unity to the vast, sparsely populated territories of Canada. As railways had fulfilled such a national objective in the time of building of the nation, broadcasting in the early twenties and thirties took on analagous significance — and the greatest successes were to be made, Thornton and others argued, if such instruments of nationhood were owned and operated by federally regulated bodies. Thornton's notion of providing radio service to passengers was realized, but only because of a co-operative arrangement of the publicly owned CNR radio stations and privately owned broadcasting outlets.

Nevertheless, emphasis upon public sector ownership of Canadian broadcasting was strong at the time, and was consistent with Thornton's view that radio was a national trust. In emphasizing the perceived threat that private commercial ownership presented to this new instrument of national unity, Thornton had stated that "it is essential that broadcasting be surrounded with such safeguards as will prevent the air becoming what might be described as an atmospheric billboard."[18]

The Royal Commission that led to the enactment of the 1932 Act was the 1929 (Aird) Commission, cited earlier. Major recommendations of that Commission parallelled the beliefs enunciated by Sir Henry Thornton:
- broadcasting should be placed on the basis of a public service
- stations providing this service should be owned by one national company
- that company should be vested with all the powers of private enterprise, and that it should function as a public utility
- the company should be empowered to purchase existing radio stations so as to fulfil the national public service purpose, and should be known as the Canadian Radio Broadcasting Company.

Subsequent to the acceptance of the Aird Commission Report, Prime Minister R. B. Bennett presented his bill concerning radio broadcasting to Parliament in May 1932. He emphasized that Canadians must be assured of complete Canadian control of broadcasting so that it would be free of foreign interference and influence:

> Without such control radio broadcasting can never become a great agency for the communication of matters of national concern and for the diffusion of national thoughts and ideals, and without such control it can never be

the agency by which national consciousness may be fostered and sustained and national unity still further strengthened.[19]

At that same time, the prime minister declared his convictions about the effect of private ownership upon a broadcasting system that would be expected to respond most directly to what he termed "the popular will and the national need." He affirmed that only public ownership could ensure to all citizens equal enjoyment of the benefits and pleasures of radio broadcasting because "private ownership must necessarily discriminate between densely and sparsely populated areas. This is not a correctable fault in private ownership; it is an inescapable and inherent demerit of the system."

The Radio Broadcasting Act of 1932 established the Canadian Radio Broadcasting Commission and empowered it to carry on the business of broadcasting in Canada. As well, that Act empowered the broadcasting commission to lease or purchase privately owned radio stations, or to make arrangments with private stations for the broadcasting of national programs. This pattern of co-operative public-private affiliation proved to be reasonably successful and was further applied when television appeared as a popular medium in Canada. The 1932 Act did not, therefore, follow through fully on the recommendations made by the Aird Report regarding public ownership.

The resistance of private broadcasters (organized by the Canadian Association of Broadcasters, established in 1926 as the voice of private broadcasting in Canada) as well as the economic circumstances of the 1930s, prevented the complete nationalization of the Canadian broadcasting system.[20] This was the case even though the public broadcasting proponents, led by the Canadian Radio League (a vocal public lobby formed in 1930) had gained respectable support for their position. The essential argument of the Radio League focused on two main points: the private ownership of radio would result in undue emphasis on business considerations rather than on the fulfilment of the national purpose; and a strong, government-owned network could best oppose the numerous high-powered American stations whose voices blanketed Canada as well as the United States.[21]

Among the many supporters of the Radio League was the Canadian newspaper industry. In 1931, the league gained positive editorial support from 27 of the nation's top circulation papers,[22] indicating that these newspapers agreed on the need for a publicly owned national system of broadcasting. Historians have confirmed what would appear to be obvious in this instance. A public broadcasting system was less likely to pose a threat to newspaper advertising revenues than would be an enlarged private commercial sector in the industry.

1936 Broadcasting Act:
Strengthening the Public Sector

Three studies by special parliamentary committees on broadcasting followed the 1932 Act, each in turn recommending the strengthening of a public broadcasting system while, at the same time, acknowledging the local service functions of privately owned stations. For example, the 1936 special parliamentary committee indicated that while in 1932 there had been 69 privately owned radio stations, in 1936 there were 73 private stations and only 8 publicly owned stations.[23] Such a lack of growth in the public sector was felt to be inconsistent with the intended direction of Canadian broadcasting policy — that is, to develop a national system of broadcasting utilizing the co-operative resources of both public and private ownership. The Canadian Radio Broadcasting Commission had failed to fulfil the intent of the Act that created it. Essentially, the commission found itself unable to reconcile the interests of private broadcasters with public interest as it has been defined. With the clamoring of the Radio League for a bill to redirect the focus of Canadian broadcasting, Parliament decided to act.

The subsequent Act passed by Parliament in 1936 created the Canadian Broadcasting Corporation (CBC), modelled in part on the British Broadcasting Corporation. The CBC was granted regulatory control over all networks and the programs and advertising of all private stations. The corporation would function, therefore, as a national broadcasting system, and in addition, would make recommendations to the government on all licensing and related matters. Thus was born the interdependent national broadcasting system, consisting of publicly and privately owned elements, that has continued to this day.

The extent to which this relationship was acceptable to both parties was another matter. The Canadian Broadcasting Corporation had to pursue its mandate for national service through private stations, whose co-operation was forced by law. In some instances the national service was welcomed by private broadcasters, while in others they complained that the compulsory CBC schedule of programs was commercially limiting. Their complaints were channelled through the Canadian Association of Broadcasters.

The CAB, located in Ottawa, was a strong influence on parliamentarians and a powerful voice for putting the case of the private broadcaster before the public. The essential problem in the broadcasting community, asserted the CAB, was that private stations were being regulated by a body that was at the same time competing with them. While the private sector had unquestionably grown during this period of regulation by the CBC, the CAB argued that the 1936 Act required clarification regarding regulatory intent: the Act lent itself to conflicting interpretations, claimed the CAB, in that it was not clear whether a public system was intended or whether a national system (made up of private and public spheres) was what legislators had in mind.

Such was the basis of arguments presented by the CAB to a public hearing of the Royal Commission on National Development in the Arts, Letters and Sciences in 1949.[24] The Massey Commission (after its chairman, Vincent Massey) had been struck by the federal government to review the effectiveness of a variety of public agencies intended to "express national feeling, promote common understanding and add to the variety and richness of Canadian life."

The CAB requested that in lieu of the CBC regulatory function, an independent regulatory agency be established over all broadcasting. The Massey Commission did not agree. Rather, they asserted that broadcasting in Canada "is a public service directed and controlled in the public interest by a body responsible to Parliament," and hence the Canadian Broadcasting Corporation should continue to be the authority controlling national broadcasting. They feared that the development of private broadcasting networks would not only destroy the national system, but that "networks of private stations would inevitably become small parts of American systems." The commission maintained that the CBC should continue its role as both broadcaster and regulator, arguing that such a system would achieve the basic objectives for Canadian broadcasting: to provide coverage of Canadian content for the entire population, offer ample opportunities for the development of Canadian artistic talents, and stimulate Canadian self-expression. At the same time, such a unified system could best provide "successful resistance to the absorption of Canada into the general cultural pattern of the United States."[25]

The CBC continued in its dual role, and, as television services were introduced in 1952, it extended its licensing and regulatory jurisdiction over the new medium as well. Where its budgets permitted (mainly in the larger regional centres), the CBC established its own stations. When public money was not available for constructing facilities, privately owned TV stations were licensed for such secondary markets on the understanding that they would carry the basic CBC network programs.

1958 Broadcasting Act:
Public and Private Ownership Roles Re-examined

The strong support the Canadian Radio League found among many of Canada's leading newspapers began to diminish following the conclusion of World War II. With the introduction of television the dissatisfaction of the Canadian Association of Broadcasters with the CBC as a regulatory agency intensified and now Canada's newspapers joined to press for another review of Canada's broadcasting system. Television was booming in the United States in the early 1950s and about half of Canada's population was well within direct reach of those US televised signals. Pressures within Parliament and in the broader community for a review of Canadian broadcasting and the directions being offered to it by the CBC continued to increase to the point where the governing Liberals could no longer deny such demands. The formation of a royal commission to review broadcasting was announced in December 1955. The terms of reference for the Commission specified objectives for Canadian broadcasting: that broadcasting should be aimed at permitting expression to Canadian ideas and aspirations, and that a broadcasting and program distribution agency should continue to be central to Canadian broadcasting policy.[26] The Commission lauded the performance of the CBC for developing Canadian talent and for overall contributions to "Canadianization" of the airwaves. In contrast it asserted that private broadcasters, for the most part, had done little to encourage Canadian talent.

While the Report emphasized the need to Canadianize programming, it also commented upon the direction that the two kinds of ownership would likely follow, given the context of a mixed system of public and private ownership:

> We cannot choose between a Canadian broadcasting system controlled by the state and a Canadian competitive system in private hands. The choice is between a Canadian state-controlled system with some flow of programmes east and west across Canada, with some Canadian content and the development of a Canadian sense of identity, at a substantial public cost, and a privately owned system which the forces of economics will necessarily make predominantly dependent on imported American radio and television programmes.[27]

The report underlined that private broadcasting was characterized by the economic pressures of the marketplace and was geared to profit-making business practices. Nevertheless, the report affirmed that private owners should be held accountable for their performances and they should be required to justify the continued grant of a valuable public franchise. The commissioners counselled private broadcasters that they "should stop worrying about the bogey of nationalization that has filled them with suspicion and fear in the past."

The central concern of the Commission was the inroads that US broadcasting content was making into Canadian society. To counteract this information flow, the Commission set forth a policy direction for a new independent regulatory body that was to be established over all Canadian broadcasting:

> If we want to have radio and television contribute to a Canadian consciousness and sense of identity, if we wish to make some part of the trade in ideas and culture move east and west across the country, if we seek to avoid engulfment by American cultural forces, we must regulate such matters as importation of programmes.[28]

The strong emphasis on the need to regulate non-Canadian content eventually found expression in the 1958 Broadcasting Act. The Act provided for a new, independent regulatory body, the Board of Broadcast Governors (BBG). The establishment of the BBG in 1958 was a victory for the private broadcasters, who had objected to the regulatory functions of the CBC since its inception. In a sense, the establishment of the BBG also represented a denial of the emphasis made by the earlier Aird Report of 1929 for a strong publicly owned broadcasting system, such as the CBC, to protect the political integrity of the nation. The BBG quickly set about its tasks of ensuring "the continued existence and efficient operation of a national broadcasting system and the provision of a varied and comprehensive broadcasting service of a high standard that is basically Canadian in content and character."[29] One of its first acts was to announce its intent to enact a Canadian content quota system for television stations, and to invite the expression of points of view on the matter from Canadian society at large.[30]

Television Content Regulations

The content regulations received a mixed reception. The Canadian Radio League argued that content regulations were essential for the creation and maintenance of a truly national broadcasting system. Its brief to the BBG public hearing on content quotas echoed one of its founders, Graham Spry, who in 1931 was one of those who regarded broadcasting as an instrument through which national unity could be achieved. The "majestic instrument" of broadcasting, Spry had emphasized, has potential, influence, and significance too vast "to be left to the petty purpose of selling soap."[31]

The Canadian Association of Broadcasters presented a brief opposing the enactment of quotas and urging instead experimentation rather than hasty implementation so as not to make "Canadian content" synonymous with mediocrity.

The judgment as to whether that warning turned out to be prophetic varies from critic to critic. However, it is fair to say that after the imposition of television content regulations in 1960, Canadian audiences, in significant numbers, turned to United States stations rather than view the struggles of a burgeoning domestic industry, which scheduled a myriad of talk shows, quiz shows, and the like so as to fulfil quota requirements. US programming was now available in many areas of the country. For example, US television was available to 50% of Quebec residents, to 77% in Ontario, 68% in Manitoba, and 84% in British Columbia.[32]

The considerable controversy surrounding the content regulations led to public commentary intended to convert members of the BBG from one view to another. Whether the regulations were successful in helping to sharpen Canadian identity, to enhance Canadian unity, or to foster the self-expression of Canadians, is debatable. Their impact is more apparent in the physical building of a television production industry, which scarcely existed prior to their enactment, since, in essence, broadcasters considered their prime function was to behave as distributors of content rather than as creators of content for any other than their own immediate needs. It appears clear, however, that the regulations failed to recapture Canadian audiences from US programming. Dr. Andrew Stewart, Chairman of the BBG, frequently noted that as citizens, Canadians publicly supported the content regulations but paradoxically, as television viewers, they often chose to view content produced in the United States rather than in Canada.[33]

Enforcement of the content regulations was difficult: violations were plentiful, more out of an inability to fulfil the regulations than in defiance of the BBG. Provisions that permitted broadcasters to calculate content from the United Kingdom and French-language countries as "domestic" occasioned accusations of favoritism toward the private broadcaster. Thus, while the technical problems in trying to make the regulations work were many, the BBG faced even more fundamental political ones.

1968 Broadcasting Act:
Redefinition of National Purposes

The 1958 Broadcasting Act, which had continued the Canadian Broadcasting Corporation establishment with its own separate Board of Directors, specified that the CBC was to operate a national broadcasting service. This condition was so vague, in terms of regulatory responsibility between the BBG and the CBC, as to invite almost certain conflict between the two structures.

In 1959 the BBG invited applications for second TV stations in areas already served by the CBC (to offer other television programming choices to Canadians). Subsequently, a second television network, the Canadian Television Network (CTV), was established in October 1961 to serve new, privately owned stations that were not affiliated with the CBC.

This development reflected the BBG's interpretation of their mandate to ensure "the continued existence and efficient operation of a national broadcasting system." Their assumption, in strengthening the position of private broadcasting in Canada, was that private stations should not be expected to function as a service peripheral to the CBC, but that all broadcasting should be part of a national system. Private broadcasters would be expected not only to fulfil a local community role, but should also make their contributions to the national purpose. BBG chairman Andrew Stewart indicated that his interpretation of the Broadcast Act differed from the CBC interpretation:

> I am bound to say, that, as we understand the position of the [Canadian Broadcasting] Corporation, the essential meaning of the Act as I have described it, and the meaning of the words of the Act as I have given them, have not been concurred in by, or acceptable to the Corporation. The position of the Corporation seems to have been that the Act doesn't mean what it says; or if it does, it shouldn't.[34]

The jurisdictional disputes between the BBG and the CBC, flowing from the 1958 Act, made it apparent in the early 1960s that there was a need for new legislation. Consequently, in May 1964, the responsible minister, Maurice Lamontagne, set up yet another new Committee on Broadcasting. Its terms of reference specified that, among other things, the committee should review the 1958 Act, and recommend amendments; appraise the operations and structure of the CBC, in particular inquiring into the relationship between the government and the CBC; and study the various means of providing alternative television services in the country.[35]

The report of the committee was issued fifteen months after the initial announcement. Its opening statement signalled the emphasis of the study: "The only thing that really matters in broadcasting is program content;

all the rest is housekeeping.'' The committee affirmed that the content regulations enacted subsequent to the 1958 Act sought to ensure that broadcasting be basically Canadian in character, but were not intended to prohibit foreign programs. Nevertheless, the report continued,

> the Canadian broadcasting system must never become a mere agency for transmitting foreign programs, however excellent they may be. A population of 20 million people surely has something of its own to say, and broadcasting is an instrument by which it must have an opportunity to express itself.[36]

With respect to the conflicts between the CBC and the BBG, it was recommended that a new Broadcasting Act provide for a new regulatory body with delegated authority over all sectors of Canadian broadcasting.

After the committee reported, the Secretary of State, Judy LaMarsh, issued a White Paper on Broadcasting in 1966 for parliamentary study. The White Paper restated the continuing resolve for a clearly identifiable Canadian political identity, and for Canadian unity, and thus the need to develop a national system of radio and television broadcasting in Canada. The White Paper argued that,

> the situation in 1966 is no different from that at any point in our history.... Any statement of policy relating to broadcasting in Canada therefore starkly poses this question. How can the people of Canada retain a degree of collective control over the new techniques of electronic communication that will be sufficient to preserve and strengthen the political, social and economic fabric of Canada, which remains the most important objective of public policy?[37]

In March 1967, the House of Commons Standing Committee on Broadcasting, Films and Assistance to the Arts issued a report on the White Paper. They concurred with the central thrust of the White Paper by emphasizing that a distinctly Canadian broadcasting system was essential to Canada's identity, unity and vitality:

> Transportation was a key factor in shaping Canada in the past. Communications will play a major role in shaping Canada of the future. It has been said that transportation is the skeleton on which the Canadian body politic has grown during the past one hundred years. In future, broadcasting may well be regarded as the central nervous system of Canadian nationhood.[38]

A revised Broadcasting Act, passed in March 1968, legislated a new regulatory body over all broadcasting matters — the Canadian Radio-television Commission (CRTC). The CRTC soon initiated more vigorous regulations directing the functioning of broadcasting as a nation-building instrument. The commission's intent was reflected in the following statement: ''The Commission is of the opinion that the Canadian broadcasting system, whose development the Commission must regulate and supervise, *must now improve rapidly or risk disappearing as a system.*''[39]

The CRTC soon began to exercise its strengthened and enlarged authority. If any Canadian broadcasters, public or private, had any doubts about what powers the CRTC had gained from the 1968 Broadcasting Act, they might well have heeded the action taken by the CRTC in respect to cable television.

Community Antenna Television had up to this point been largely unregulated. As program distributors rather than as broadcasters, licences for them had been issued by the federal minister of transport. Under the CRTC, this no longer would be the case. As with conventional broadcasters, licensing and relicensing would no longer be automatic, but would necessitate public hearings at which qualifications would be scrutinized before any licensing action was taken. All broadcasting in the country would henceforth be considered as a single system, each part with a designated role to play, so as to avoid the "Americanization of the Canadian consciousness."[40] Broadcasting, emphasized the Commission "is not an end... It is subject to higher and more general imperatives of national development and survival."[41] This attitude on the part of the CRTC captured the spirit of early broadcast critics and, although it did not meet their goal of a largely publicly owned system, it did provide for a working partnership of both the public and private sectors.

The CRTC had stated from the start of its existence that Canadians must enlarge their communication system quantitatively and qualitatively. In the absence of such growth, particularly of programming production resources (television, radio, and film), Canada would end up having "a technically sophisticated distribution system for imported programs."[42]

The need to develop more programming content was indicated in February 1970, when the CRTC announced its intent to boost the Canadian quota requirement for television stations from 55 to 60 percent.[43] As well, programs from any one foreign country would be limited to 30 percent of any television schedule, a regulation obviously aimed at curtailing the flow of United States content into Canada.

Regulations for content quotas in the radio industry were equally important. Within eight months, the announcement indicated, a minimum of 30 percent of musical compositions broadcast by radio stations, during certain specified daily periods, would have to meet Canadian production criteria (the musical composition, the writing of lyrics, the playing and singing, and place of production) in a phased-in manner over a period of several years.

This requirement of Canadian music triggered a rapid expansion in the recording industry, which "seemed to develop overnight."[44] In one year in Toronto, the recording capability of 16-track studios increased from one studio to six. Most Canadian radio stations, several of which had claimed earlier that Canadian talent was not to be found, were soon broadcasting in excess of the 30 percent requirement.

Perhaps, as some have suggested, a single "identity" for a country as large as Canada is impossible except in the most general terms. Nevertheless, the CRTC intent was clear. The identity problem was crucial to Canada's cultural survival. It was of national scope and demanded the participation of other national agencies (the CBC, the National Film Board, and, ultimately, the Canadian Film Development Corporation) to ensure that the programming materials that would eventually result from Canada's developing production industry would reflect the indigenous society rather than being "copies of a product whose basic design and concept originated in another country."[45]

To further the domestication of the industry, the Secretary of State in September 1968 issued a directive to the CRTC that offered the CRTC firm guidelines on the question of foreign ownership of Canadian broadcasting. The guideline reduced permissable foreign ownership to 20 percent of voting shares and stipulated that directors of any broadcasting company be Canadian citizens.[46] Reducing US ownership proved to be more of a problem than anticipated, because new Canadian owners were not always easy to find and those who bid for American-owned licences were often large corporations with communications holdings that were already substantial. The threat of concentration of ownership was becoming rapidly more pronounced and this evoked common concern at different times from both Andrew Stewart, chairman of the earlier BBG, and Pierre Juneau, chairman of the newly structured CRTC.[47] They agreed on the importance of private broadcasters being able to fulfil the demands of the Canadian content regulations and being still solvent enough to afford quality productions that would attract (or re-attract) Canadian audiences. On the other hand, permitting concentrated ownership as a strong financial basis for the industry threatened a needed plurality of expression.

This industrial paradox is yet to be resolved. The licensing and re-licensing of broadcasting outlets continues to be a matter of trying to distinguish between broadcasters whose concerns are basically investment oriented and those who indicate a preparedness to support the national purposes outlined in the Broadcasting Act. On the other hand, the difficulty for broadcasters has been the making of "good business" congruent with "good Canadianism." Thus, evaluations of "promises of performance" (commitments made regarding programming) have become a dominant feature of all CRTC licensing procedures. Accordingly, broadcaster "accountability" to society has been introduced as a criterion of who should be entrusted to operate within Canada's broadcasting system.

The Publishing Industry

Canada's print media have been free from the control that has surrounded broadcasting from its earliest days. Newspapers are relatively free to pursue their own political directions, in support of, or in opposition to, whichever politician or party appeals to the tradition, persuasion, or whim of the newspaper publisher or editor. Despite such relative freedom to function unfettered, even during election periods, while unencumbered by any legislated mandate to pursue specific national purposes, Canada's news publishing media have come under the close scrutiny of several formal studies.

One of these, the Massey Commission, in 1951 noted that all of the great cultural institutions in the United States are freely placed at the disposal of Canadians, to the point where "we use various American information services as if they were our own."[48] With reference to newspapers, this had led to the lamentable situation where most Canadians are little aware that a large proportion of the international news that their own community newspaper provides has been gathered and written by Americans. Canadians' view of the rest of the world is generally neither interpreted for them by other Canadians nor in the light of Canadian perspectives. The same report warned that the "closest approximation to a national literature" that Canadians have, their periodical magazine press, is financially threatened by the massive importation of foreign magazines.

Similar concerns were reiterated by the Royal Commission on Publications, which reported in 1966. The political responsibility borne by the periodical press was summarized by the Commission as it examined national tasks:

> National unity has been our chief task since Sir John A. Macdonald went about the business of building, from bickering and scattered colonies, a great transcontinental nation. Sir Wilfrid Laurier continued it when he strove to bring French and English closer together under a common crown. … The role of the periodical press in building this Canadian unity cannot be ignored. But it cannot contribute its share if it is beset by overwhelming competitive conditions that threaten its existence.[49]

Studies on the role of the media seem to come as regularly as the Census, and thus the Special Senate Committee on Mass Media repeated these concerns in 1970. The federal government subsequently moved to protect Canada's magazine industry by amending the Income Tax Act in 1976. No tax deductions would be allowed for advertisements placed in non-Canadian magazines — and, to qualify for Canadian status, it became necessary for a publication to generate most of its content domestically. Rather than comply with the requirement for Canadian status, Time Incorporated ceased its Canadian publication. The net result of the amendment was that Canadian advertising dollars that had normally been flowing to foreign publications (for example, to *Time* and *Reader's Digest*) were redirected to Canadian publications.

Rather than foreign competition, concentrated ownership became the major issue with respect to newspapers. While no conclusive evidence supports the contention that large corporate ownership of newspapers results in editorial manipulation of a newspaper,[50] the inevitable consequence of amalgamations or the abandonment of a market is fewer editorial voices. A paradox emerges: Canadian newspapers tend to espouse the libertarian view that multiple competing editorial voices are likely to reveal truths, but their very functioning, given free reign for competitive economics to run its course, eliminates newspaper competition. The public interest is thus ill served. According to, among others, the 1970 Special Senate Committee on Mass Media, "The desire to have a voice in ordering the institutions that govern our lives is a universal human constant.... The more separate voices we have telling us what's going on..., the more effectively we can govern ourselves."[51]

For the first time, firm recommendations emanated from a formal study asking for controls on the publishing industry to stem the economic forces which lead to concentration. The committee report emphasized that, while some expansions of media holdings may have benefited the public interest, others have not. It concluded that the principle has been already established "that the state has a right to safeguard the public's right to information by approving, disapproving, or disallowing various property transactions within the broadcasting industry. The Committee believes it is time for this principle to be extended to include the print media."[52]

Few of the Senate committee's recommendations were adopted. Its call for Press Councils to be established met with some regional success, but the practice did not become national in scope. Moreover, the recommendation that a Press Ownership Review Board be established to determine whether the public interest would be harmed by further amalgamations or take-overs of newspapers was not popularly received by either media industries or government.

The simultaneous closing, on 27 August 1980, of the Winnipeg *Tribune* and the Ottawa *Journal* (owned, respectively, by Southam Press Limited and by Thomson Newspapers Limited) reminded Canadians of the consequences of the absence of any formal review activity. Within a week of those closings, a Royal Commission on Newspapers (the Kent Commission) was formed to review the newspaper industry in Canada and to report on "the degree to which the present situation in the newspaper industry has affected or might affect fulfilment of the newspaper industry's responsibilities to the public."[53] One of the prime recommendations of the commission was that the government enact a Canada Newspaper Act designed "to secure for the press of Canada the freedom that is essential to a democratic society." The freedom to which the report referred was freedom from interference from government restraints as well as from restraints imposed by minority and commercial interests and pressures.

While newspapers have been urged to accept nation-building roles, moral suasion has not as yet been translated into legal directives, such as those suggested by the Kent Commission. During election campaigns it is apparent that Canada's newspapers do not hesitate to act as advocates of particular candidates or parties. Indeed, in the 1979 federal election, nearly half of a sample of twenty-three Canadian newspapers endorsed one of the three major parties in their editorial columns, and none offered "equal space" for commentary from opposing parties.

Regulation of Broadcasting during Election Campaigns

With respect to broadcasting a totally different set of conditions apply. Radio and television coverage of campaigns and controversial commentary are controlled in considerable detail. Rather than functioning in the traditional framework of journalism, broadcasting functions within guidelines have developed from concerns about the social responsibility of the broadcast media.

The Canadian Broadcasting Act of 1932 made no mention of political programming, but simply outlined the broad powers of the Canadian Radio Broadcasting Commission over the regulation of broadcasting and its powers to carry on the business of broadcasting. The 1936 Broadcasting Act, however, charged the Canadian Broadcasting Corporation with the responsibility to prescribe time periods to be devoted to political broadcasts (by privately owned stations as well as those owned by the Corporation) and to ensure that such times were assigned equitably to all parties and candidates. Further, the Act stipulated that sponsors of political broadcasts were to be identified, and "dramatized" political commentary was banned. These were the first explicit instructions and prohibitions concerning political broadcasts. Previously, arrangements for carrying political programming had been by informal agreements between stations and parties or candidates. The regulatory authority at the time, the Canadian Radio Broadcasting Commission, became involved only when permission was required for networking.

The conditions for election broadcasts did not find their way into the regulatory process by accident. In the 1935 federal election, the R. B. Bennett Conservatives had designed a campaign that included attacks against Liberal leader Mackenzie King. Arousing the Liberals' ire in particular were dramatized radio broadcasts that used a voice character who was identified only as "Mr. Sage."[54] These dramatizations, labelled libelous by the Liberals, proved to be the last of their kind, and strict controls over dramatization in programs of a partisan political nature were initiated by the successful Liberals following that 1935 election. Such controls, with modifications, continue to this day.

It was the Canadian Broadcasting Corporation that clarified the broadcasting media's code of behavior during election campaigns and with regard to controversial broadcasting between elections. It provided a philosophical basis that (through its successor bodies, the BBG and the CRTC) has continued to serve today. In formal statements in 1939, amended in 1944, and again in 1948, [55] the CBC enunciated guidelines founded upon concepts of free speech and the right to reply that are integral to a free, democratic society.

Charging advertising rates for political broadcasts, affirmed the CBC, does not serve the political process well. All parties must be offered equal and fair opportunities to explain their positions on issues of the moment. Several other principles were equally firmly enunciated: the airwaves belong to the people — therefore, they are a public rather than a private commodity; no one by virtue of position or wealth should be permitted to dominate the airwaves; and the right to respond to ideas is inherent in the concept of free speech.

The 1958 Broadcast Act merely reiterated the provisions of the 1936 Act regarding political broadcasting, but the 1968 Act outlined the purpose of political broadcasting:

- all persons licensed to carry on broadcasting undertakings have a responsibility for programs they broadcast but the right to freedom of expression and the right of persons to receive programs, subject only to generally applicable statutes and regulations, is unquestioned;
- the programing provided by the Canadian broadcasting system should be varied and comprehensive and should provide reasonable, balanced opportunity for the expression of differing views on matters of public concern...[56]

In 1961 the BBG issued the *White Paper on Political and Controversial Broadcasting Policies*. Its purpose was to ensure that broadcasting would remain at the disposal of the nation, since, "for the proper functioning of representative government at all levels, it is essential that the public should be fully informed of the issues at stake in any election, and of the views and policies of the various parties toward those issues."[57] The White Paper also detailed four principles that reflect the earlier policies of the Canadian Broadcasting Corporation:

1. The air belongs to the people, who are entitled to hear the principal points of view on all questions of importance.
2. The air must not fall under the control of any individual or groups influenced by reason of their wealth or special position.
3. The right to answer is inherent in the doctrine of free speech.
4. The full interchange of opinion is one of the principal safeguards of free institutions.[58]

As well, it concurred with earlier arguments of the CBC that these principles were not well served by the sale of time to individuals or political parties.

The conduct of political broadcasts is extensively controlled. There are regulations governing such matters as advertising and selling time, identification of parties and sponsors, the broadcasting of election results, the allocation of time to candidates and parties and the right to respond. The evolution of these detailed regulations has been directed toward conforming to the four principles cited above. Some examples of this developmental process should shed light on the meticulousness of Canadian regulatory agencies in trying to keep broadcasting consistent with principles of democratic electoral conduct.

Fairness

In 1968, the CRTC ruled that a broadcasting personality who chose to run for political office while continuing a broadcasting career would receive an "inequitable advantage" over other candidates. To resolve the conflict either opposing candidates for office would have to be offered similar facilities, or the broadcaster-candidate would be required to discontinue the broadcasting career until after the election.[59] In another case a by-election had been called for York West for 16 October 1972. The Liberal candidate was an employee of CFTO-TV in Toronto, and had been nominated by his riding in advance of the issuance of the election writ. The CRTC ruled that during the formally declared campaign period, the broadcaster-candidate would need to suspend his broadcasting activities, though he could continue them up to that point.[60] In a similar instance, a broadcaster-candidate was permitted to continue with his career activities in the pre-election period, so long as in his on-air performances he did not broadcast material of a partisan nature in relation to an election.[61]

These rulings are a manifestation of the concern for fairness. Canadian regulations in broadcasting do not contain what in the United States has been labelled the *Fairness Doctrine*. In that country, broadcasters are obliged not only to operate on a basis of fairness with respect to public issues, but are required to "afford reasonable opportunity for the discussion of conflicting views on issues of public importance."[62] The letter and spirit of the Canadian regulations, as evidenced in the four principles cited earlier, support identical concerns. Basic to both nations is an understanding that in matters of public debate, the broadcaster has a unique responsibility "as a fiduciary — a trustee of the public interest."[63]

Broadcast Editorials

While editorial content of a controversial nature has been encouraged, broadcasters have been required to announce that persons who have a different view are permitted the right of response.[64] This differs dramatically from newspapers' traditions on matters of public controversy. While newspapers are not compelled to do so, most out of concern for the principle of freedom to respond make generous efforts to publish letters submitted by their reading public. This is not required by law. Even in broadcasting, the CRTC has recognized that in some instances it becomes impossible to describe or present all sides of an issue. For example, the Commission has argued, "it would be patently ridiculous requiring a program attacking air pollution to be balanced with a program lauding such a condition." Nevertheless, it is mandatory that even issues that tend to be unidimensional with respect to public attitudes must be dealt with fairly and honestly and must be clearly represented as controversial, if such is the case.[65]

During elections, however, editorial comment has been stringently regulated. Indeed, even news commentary, which lends itself to partisan interpretation, has been monitored. This led some stations to keep a day-by-day tally of the length of news stories about political parties to ensure that, during the official campaign period, none enjoyed more comment than another. Moreover, for over 25 years, stations have been prohibited from broadcasting a program, advertisement, or comment of a political character in relation to a referendum, or a municipal, provincial, or federal election, on election day or the day previous.

This prohibition has recently been modified and the two-day blackout period now refers only to partisan political advertising (paid for or donated) and does not limit broadcasters with respect to programs under their editorial control.[66] This change was accompanied by a reminder that broadcasters were obligated, nonetheless, to observe the demands of the Broadcasting Act, which specifies that programming should be "varied and comprehensive and should provide reasonable, balanced opportunity for the expression of differing views on matters of public concern."[67]

Allocation of Party Broadcast Time during Elections

It has not been easy to regulate, to everyone's satisfaction, the allocation of broadcast time to political parties during elections.

The CRTC criteria to determine the eligibility of political parties for free time, for example, were found in 1970 to contravene the Quebec Election Act.[68] Nevertheless, it appears that the current system of time allocation is satisfactory. Representatives of political parties represented in the House of Commons meet with the broadcasting industry, the Chief Electoral Officer, and the CRTC to determine time schedules and amounts. If agreement cannot be reached, the matter is referred to the CRTC for resolution. Current regulations also provide time for parties that are not represented in the House of Commons.

The distribution pattern utilized for the 1980 federal election demonstrates the attempt to provide fair treatment to parties and candidates.[69] For that election each broadcaster was expected to make available six-and-one-half hours of prime broadcast time, accomplished by stations either as independent operations or as network affiliate stations. Based on this requirement, time was allocated for purchase in the following amounts: Progressive Conservative Party — 143 minutes (36.67% of the six-and-a-half hours); Liberal Party — 137 minutes (35.13%); New Democratic Party — 64 minutes (16.40%); Social Credit Party — 22 minutes (5.64%); Communist Party — 6 minutes (1.54%); Libertarian Party — 6 minutes (1.54%); Marxist-Leninist Party — 6 minutes (1.54%); Parti Rhinoceros — 6 minutes (1.54%).

The regulations stipulated that free-time periods would also be made available to parties and that the allocations would be made in the same proportionate amounts as the six-and-a-half hours of purchased time. These free time periods were to be available from networks in these amounts: CBC-AM (English) — 2 hours; CBC-AM (French) — 2 hours; Radiomutuel — 1 hour; Telemedia — 1 hour; CBC-TV (English) — 3½ hours; CBC-TV (French) — 3½ hours; TVA Quebec — 1 hour. The political parties themselves could determine presentation formats for their allocated time.

While stations were permitted to make time available to any individual candidate additional to the designated party time allocation cited above, if they did so, they were required to make these arrangements through the offices of registered party agents and to make known to other candidates that equitable time was also available to them.

As well, continuing past practice, stations were required to identify clearly on whose behalf broadcasts were made. Further, all such political election broadcasting was to be included in detail on station logs, which would eventually be forwarded to the CRTC for perusal as records of performance.

The flexibility accorded political parties to use their time as they saw fit has confirmed the use of commercial spot announcements in political campaigns in Canada. Since their earliest use by Dwight D. Eisenhower, the Republican nominee in the 1952 US Presidential campaign, they have been a source of concern and public complaints. Critics of such advertising-agency-designed campaigns in both countries argue that it is impossible in twenty or thirty seconds to discuss or explain vital and complex social issues. Spot campaigns, they complain, become devoted to "image" politics and candidate "packaging" at the expense of social debate. Further, critics claim that such campaigning has taken the election campaign out of the hands of politicians and politically active citizens, and placed it into the domain of professional hucksters and their advertising agencies, all in a context where marketing-advertising practices prevail over more fundamental concerns.

Cable Television (CATV) Systems

The involvement of CATV systems in the political campaign process has not been ignored by the CRTC. Regulation for CATV conduct during election campaigns emphasize that, generally, CATV systems are prohibited from carrying political advertising except when this is permitted as a special condition of licence. As well, CATV systems are under no obligation to become involved in political programming with respect to elections.

If cable systems choose to transmit political programming, they are obliged to respect the principles that conventional broadcasters must observe. For example, programming of a partisan political nature is confined to the twenty-nine days before the election, when advertising is permissible. As well, the CATV station, if it makes time available to any party or candidate, it is obliged to offer time on an equitable basis to competing parties and candidates.

Release of Election Results

Section 105 of the Canada Elections Act explicitly forbids the premature publication or release of election results:

> No person, company or corporation shall, in any electoral district before the hour fixed by or pursuant to this Act for the closing of the polls in that electoral district, publish the result or purported result of the polling in any electoral district in Canada by radio or television broadcast, by newspaper, newssheet, poster, billboard or hand bill or in any other manner.[70]

The prohibition has been in effect for many years, and was designed to prevent voters in one part of the country from being influenced by results elsewhere. Thus while newsroom personnel in western Canada, through their wire services, have exact details regarding who won and who lost in the eastern provinces, they are prohibited from releasing those results while voting is still underway in their own areas. As satellite distribution technology develops, it will be increasingly difficult to enforce this prohibition.

Conclusion

This chapter has discussed media roles in the political process of an open democratic society. Canadian society has developed extensive expectations that are different from those of other open societies. These are reflected in a history of regulatory efforts to harness Canada's media resources so as to foster and maintain a clearly distinguishable social and political national identity and consciousness.

Often these regulatory efforts have sought to develop cultural activities in the country, and have been associated with various strategies for "domesticating" media content. Much of our discussion has centred on these concerns rather than specifically on how media cover an election. Nonetheless, this has been done for a specific purpose. We believe it is important to view media operations within the framework that offers a focus for all media activities — that is the striving that Canadian society has made for a clearly identifiable political entity. To have done less than has been discussed here would have offered an imbalanced view of the regulatory processes as these developed historically to include all media as they perform political tasks directly (in elections) and indirectly, between elections.

Notes

[1]For a detailed discussion and concise examination of the relationship of mass media within particular political systems, see Fred. S. Siebert, Theodore Peterson, and Wilbur Schramm, *Four Theories of the Press* (Urbana, Illinois: University of Illinois Press, 1973).

[2]For an account of the struggle between the "business" and "news" departments of the Washington *Post*, see David Halberstam, *The Powers That Be* (New York: Dell Publishing, 1980), pp. 745-9.

[3]On the development of social responsibility theory, which is described as "largely a grafting of new ideas onto traditional theory," see Theodore Peterson, "The Social Responsibility Theory of the Press," in Siebert, Peterson, and Schramm, *Four Theories of the Press*, pp. 73-103; see also Arthur Siegel, *Politics and the Media in Canada* (Toronto: McGraw-Hill Ryerson, 1983), p. 17.

[4]On this point see, Edwin R. Black and Alan C. Cairns, "A Different Perspective on Canadian Federalism," *Canadian Public Administration*, 9

(March 1966) and J.M.S. Careless, "'Limited Identities' in Canada," *Canadian Historical Review*, 50 (March 1969).

[5] For a detailed study of the birth and development of the British Broadcasting Corporation, see Walter B. Emery, *National and International Systems of Broadcasting* (East Lansing, Michigan: Michigan State University Press, 1969), pp. 81-108.

[6] Communications Canada, *Report of the Federal Cultural Policy Review Committee* (Ottawa: Supply and Services Canada, 1982).

[7] Harry J. Boyle (Vice-Chairman, Canadian Radio-television Commission), an address to the Second National Conference of Journalists, Ottawa, 11 March 1972.

[8] Robert L. Perry, "Industrial Gaps Left as U.S. Withdraws," *Financial Post*, 25 (April 1981), p. 20.

[9] Ibid.

[10] Edward Broadbent, "On Independence and Socialism," *The Canadian Forum*, 52 (April 1972), 31.

[11] This preference continues to be evident. For example, the CRTC pointed out in 1982 that 70% of the viewing time of English-language television is spent watching non-Canadian programs. For French-language television, the corresponding figure is 39%. See CRTC *Facts Digest on Broadcasting and Telecommunication in Canada* (Ottawa: CRTC, 1982), p. 10. Data collected by the Special Senate Committee on Mass Media in Canada in the late 1960s revealed that Canadians spent as much money purchasing *Playboy* magazine as they did on the 17 largest English-language Canadian consumer magazines combined. Further, Canadians spent more money buying American comic books than they did on the 17 leading Canadian-owned magazines. See *Report of the Special Senate Committee on Mass Media: The Uncertain Mirror*, Volume I (Ottawa: Information Canada, 1970), p. 156. Reprinted in 1975.

[12] Canada, *Report of the Royal Commission on Radio Broadcasting 1929* (Ottawa: The King's Printer, 1929).

[13] Communications Canada, *Proposals for a Communications Policy for Canada* (Ottawa: Information Canada, 1963).

[14] Ibid., p. 8.

[15] See Frank W. Peers, *The Politics of Canadian Broadcasting 1920-1951* (Toronto: University of Toronto Press, 1969), p. 16.

[16] Ibid., p. 17.

[17] D'Arcy Marsh, *The Tragedy of Henry Thornton* (Toronto, 1935), pp. 115-6, cited by Peers, p. 24.

[18] Henry Thornton (President of the Canadian National Railway), an address to the Advertising Clubs of the World, Philadelphia, 21 June 1926. See details and citation in Ernest A. Weir, *The Struggle for National Broadcasting in Canada* (Toronto: McClelland and Stewart, 1965), p. 17.

[19] Canada, House of Commons, *Debates of the House of Commons Seventeenth Parliament*, Volume 3, May 18, 1932 (Ottawa: The King's Printer, 1932), p. 3035.

[20] Canada, The Senate, *Report of the Special Senate Committee on Mass Media the Uncertain Mirror*, Volume I, p. 194. Weir, pp. 126-9, describes the support private broadcasters found from the example of the Canadian Pacific Railway, a private corporation that had strong aspirations about entering the broadcasting industry.

[21]John Egli O'Brien, "A History of the Canadian Radio League: 1930-1936," unpublished Ph.D. dissertation, University of Southern California, 1964, pp. 105-14.

[22]Peers, p. 77.

[23]Ibid., p. 185.

[24]Canada, Report of the Royal Commission on National Development in the Arts, Letters and Sciences 1949-1951 (Ottawa: The King's Printer, 1951), p. 283.

[25]Ibid., pp. 40-1.

[26]Canada, Report of the Royal Commission on Broadcasting (Ottawa: The Queen's Printer, 1957), pp. 293-4. For a detailed discussion of the events that led up to announcing the establishment of the Royal Commission, see Frank W. Peers, The Public Eye: Television and the Politics of Canadian Broadcasting 1952-1968 (Toronto: University of Toronto Press, 1979), pp. 55-64.

[27]Canada, Report of the Royal Commission on Broadcasting, 1957, p. 10.

[28]Ibid., p. 110.

[29]Canada, Canadian Broadcasting Act (Ottawa: The Queen's Printer, 1958), p. 10.

[30]See Canada, Board of Broadcast Governors, Announcement Regarding Radio (TV) Broadcast Regulations November 18, 1959 (Ottawa: Board of Broadcast Governors, 1959), p. 2. Also see Canada, Board of Broadcast Governors, Proposed Television Broadcasting Station Regulations July 28, 1959 (Ottawa: Board of Broadcast Governors, 1959).

[31]Graham Spry, "A Case for Nationalized Broadcasting," Queen's Quarterly, 38 (Winter 1931), p. 169.

[32]Canada, Report of the Committee on Broadcasting 1965 (Ottawa: The Queen's Printer, 1965), p. 35.

[33]Andrew Stewart (Chairman of the Board of Broadcast Governors), an address to the Canadian Club of Ottawa, 18 April 1962.

[34]Andrew Stewart (Chairman of the Board of Broadcast Governors), an address to the Annual Meeting of the Canadian Association of Broadcasters, 3 May 1963.

[35]Canada, Report of the Committee on Broadcasting 1965, p. vii.

[36]Ibid., p. 31.

[37]Canada, Secretary of State, White Paper on Broadcasting 1966 (Ottawa: The Queen's Printer, 1966), p. 5.

[38]Canada, House of Commons Standing Committee on Broadcasting, Films and Assistance to the Arts, Report on the White Paper on Broadcasting 1966 (Ottawa: The Queen's Printer, 1967), p. 4.

[39]Canada, Canadian Radio-television Commission, Public Announcement: The Improvement and Development of Canadian Broadcasting and the Extension of U.S. Television Coverage in Canada by CATV, December 3, 1969 (Ottawa: CRTC, 1969). (Emphasis added.)

[40]Canada, Canadian Radio-television Commission, Annual Report 1969-70 (Ottawa: CRTC, 1970), p. 5.

[41]Canada, Canadian Radio-television Commission, Annual Report 1970-71 (Ottawa: CRTC, 1971), p. 3.

[42]Canada, Canadian Radio-television Commission, Canadian Broadcasting

"A Single System": Policy Statement on Cable Television July 16, 1971 (Ottawa: CRTC, 1971), p. 37.

[43]Canada, Canadian Radio-television Commission, *Press Release: Television Programs, February 12, 1970* (Ottawa: CRTC, 1970).

[44]Canada, Canadian Radio-television Commission, *Annual Report 1970-71*, pp. 8-11.

[45]Canada, Canadian Radio-television Commission, *Canadian Broadcasting "A Single System,"* p. 40.

[46]Canada, Secretary of State, *Direction to the Radio-television Commission Pursuant to Section 27 of the Broadcasting Act, P.C. 1969-2229, November 20, 1969* (Ottawa: The Queen's Printer, 1969), Sections 3, 4. It should be noted that the 20% figure with respect to permissible foreign ownership in Canada is the same as the foreign ownership permissible in the United States.

[47]See Andrew Stewart (Chairman of the Board of Broadcast Governors) in testimony before the Canadian Senate Committee on Transport and Communications, 20 February 1968, cited in Canada, The Senate, *Report of the Special Senate Committee on Mass Media: Words, Music, and Dollars,* Volume II (Ottawa: Information Canada, 1970), p. 6. Also see Pierre Juneau, Chairman of the Canadian Radio-television Commission, an address to the Canadian Cable Television Association, Quebec City, 14 May 1969.

[48]Canada, *Report of the Royal Commission on National Development in the Arts, Letters and Sciences* (Ottawa: The King's Printer, 1951), p. 14.

[49]Canada, *Report of the Royal Commission on Publication 1961* (Ottawa: The Queen's Printer, 1961), p. 75.

[50]For example, see Canada, Royal Commission on Corporate Concentration, *Study Number 23: The Newspaper Firm and Freedom of Information* (Ottawa: Supply and Services Canada, 1977), p. 89. This study, which examined the relationship between the newspaper *La Presse* and its corporate parent Power Corporation, concluded that various factors discouraged direct or indirect interventions by owners in the newspapers journalistic activities. The study added, though, that "if, however, owners and management rarely attempt to influence the content of news, due to their sense of social and professional responsibility, or because of in-house or external counterbalancing factors, as appears to be the case with *La Presse,* it would be unwise to conclude without further analysis that the concentration of ownership or economic concentration in the print medium should cease to be a cause for concern."

[51]Canada, The Senate, *Report of the Special Senate Committee on Mass Media: The Uncertain Mirror,* Volume I, p. 3.

[52]Ibid., p. 68.

[53]*Royal Commission on Newspapers* (Ottawa: Minister of Supply and Services Canada, 1981), p. 259.

[54]For details concerning the Liberal-Conservative campaign of 1935 and of the "Mr. Sage" incident, see Frank W. Peers, *The Politics of Canadian Broadcasting,* pp. 164-7.

[55]Canada, Canadian Broadcasting Corporation, *A Statement of Policy of the Canadian Broadcasting Corporation with Respect to Controversial Broadcasting* (Ottawa: Canadian Broadcasting Corporation, 1939). Also see Canada, Canadian Broadcasting Corporation, *Political and Controversial Broadcasting: Policies and Rulings* (Ottawa: Canadian Broadcasting Corporation, 1948).

[56]Canada, *Canadian Broadcasting Act* (Ottawa: The Queen's Printer, 1968), s. 2. (c), (d). (Emphasis added.)

[57]Canada, Board of Broadcast Governors, *White Paper on Political and Controversial Broadcasting Politices December 18, 1961* (Ottawa: Board of Broadcast Governors, 1961).

[58]Ibid.

[59]Canada, Canadian Radio-television Commission, *Announcement: Broadcasters as Political Candidates May 24, 1968* (Ottawa: CRTC, 1968).

[60]Canada, Canadian Radio-television Commission, *Announcement: Broadcasters as Political Candidates July 17, 1972* (Ottawa: CRTC, 1972).

[61]Ibid.

[62]For a detailed discussion of the development of the doctrine, see Sydney W. Head, *Broadcasting in America: A Survey of Radio and Television*, 3rd. ed. (Boston: Houghton Mifflin, 1976), pp. 398-400.

[63]Ibid., p. 400.

[64]Canada, Board of Broadcast Governors, *White Paper on Political and Controversial Broadcasting Policies December 18, 1961* (Ottawa: Board of Broadcast Governors, 1961).

[65]Canada, Canadian Radio-television Commission, *Excerpts from the Report of the Special Committee on "Air of Death" July 9, 1970* (Ottawa: CRTC, 1970).

[66]Canada, Canadian Radio-television and Telecommunications Commission, *Public Announcement: Notice to Broadcasters Federal General Election CRTC Guidelines* (Ottawa: CRTC, 2 February 1978), p. 7.

[67]Ibid.

[68]CRTC, *Annual Report 1969-1970*, p. 40. Also see CRTC, *Annual Report 1970-1971*, pp. 50-1.

[69]This is intended to serve as an example only. Details regarding time distribution patterns are prone to change from election to election. See Canada, Canadian Radio-television and Telecommunications Commission, *Broadcasting Guidelines Federal General Elections, 18 February 1980, Circular No. 257* (Ottawa: CRTC, January 1980), pp. 3-9. This document has served the authors as a basis for discussion of regulations as these apply to broadcasting at times of elections and for controversial broadcasting.

[70]Section 105 of the Canada Elections Act is cited in Canada, Canadian Radio-television and Telecommunications Commission, *Circular 251* (Ottawa: CRTC, May 1979), p. 1. The CRTC reminder about this premature release of election information continues with an example: "If a radio or television station's signal is receivable in an area which is in a later time zone than the one in which the transmitter is located, there is a danger of premature publication of election results. The licensee of such radio or television station would be well advised not to transmit any election results until 9:00 p.m. in the time zone where the station's broadcast transmitter is located."

6

Major Issues Relating to Media and Politics in Canada

There is reason to think our capacity for technological innovation in communicating information has outstripped our ability to understand and to control fully the impact of our inventions. We have, for instance, made a staggering amount of information instantaneously available to ourselves, yet we are unsure whether we will be better off for it. In comparison with the early decades of the century, both the amount of political information and the means by which it reaches the public have changed enormously. At no time is this more evident than during election campaigns. Writing as we are for publication in 1984, we cannot avoid recalling George Orwell's vision of a society politically controlled by means of mass communications technology. We can today afford to dismiss such dangers even less than in the past, partly because covert and overt surveillance technology has achieved extremely high levels of sophistication. As well, technological processes are increasingly involved in information preparation. This text, for example, is the result of the application of new technologies in data accumulation, computer analysis, word processing, editing, and typesetting that scholars a few decades ago could not even have imagined.

We conclude our data presentations and discussions with some reflections on the role of Canadian media in handling political information during elections. We do not intend here to reiterate conclusions regarding gatekeeping and agenda-setting, but rather to touch on a number of media-related issues that either have emerged from our studies or are logical extensions of them.

The "Americanization" of Canadian Elections

We will begin by examining a paradox. Over the past 50 years, as we have pointed out in the preceding chapter, the dominant concern of

Canadian media regulation has unquestionably been the insulation of the Canadian public from the powerful assimilative impact of American radio and television programming. Within this context, the area of political information has been, naturally enough, of special concern, because the survival of Canada as a sovereign state was seen as depending on the maintenance of a distinctively Canadian form of social and political expression.

It might seem that since national elections are a quintessential Canadian political act (Americans don't participate in Canadian general elections, nor do they usually pay much media attention to them)[1] American influence would be least evident in this area of Canadian life. Ironically, many would argue American electoral processes, political spectacles that large numbers of Canadians follow avidly, have led to a growing Americanization of our electoral campaigns.[2]

Has there been an Americanization of the Canadian political process or are there clear alternative influences at work? Some would argue (with a great deal of validity) that the political process is not necessarily "American" or uniquely "Canadian." The political process is a product of a homogeneous North American society, not a product of separate cultures divided simply by the 49th parallel.[3] Further, arguments are heard that mass media content of any sort, whether it is produced in the United States, Canada, or elsewhere, is simply a product of the technical environment in which it is produced. A television camera, for example, has only given capabilities whether the studio is in Toronto, Vancouver, New York, or Los Angeles. This reflection leads us directly to focus on the impact that Marshall McLuhan has made on the contemporary electronic information society — that is, the medium, or the form, gives meaning to content. Nevertheless, insofar as the Canadian-American relationship is concerned, Canadian television is, in fact, dominated by US production styles and formats rather than by any indigenous, uniquely Canadian style. One need only to look at Canadian television program schedules and review their titles to determine their origins.

Whether due to the direct or indirect penetration of American political style or to the unique characteristics of television, nowhere is the change in the style of Canadian campaigning more apparent than in the concentration on leadership. This is quite natural in the United States, where the president embodies the executive branch of government and is meant to be one of the pillars (along with Congress and the courts) of a constitutional system of checks and balances. In Canada the prime minister is, at least in theory, merely the leader of a cabinet that is collectively responsible to the elected legislative body, the House of Commons. Nonetheless, modern electoral contests, abetted by television especially, have concentrated attention on those aspiring prime ministers, the party leaders, almost as if they were elected directly like the US president, rather than being dependent on winning a majority of separate parliamentary contests in 282 constituencies.

This is not to suggest that leadership is unimportant in Canadian politics. On the contrary, the party leader has always attracted intense interest, and political parties have customarily built their appeals to the electorate around their leaders. Such leadership oriented slogans as "Better Sir John A. drunk than George Brown sober" and, more prosaically, "King or chaos" are illustrations of this. But only with the modern era did this reach the level where the individual candidates for parliament (of whom after all the party leader is but one) have been relegated to a relatively insignificant role in media election coverage.

In the early years, Canadians seemed content with party leaders (chosen in caucus rather than in national convention) whose virtues might have been more evident to the political elite than to the public at large. Charisma was a quality largely lacking at the leadership level of federal politics from the day Laurier left office until John Diefenbaker arrived. During that period, Canada's national leaders gave a new meaning to the word drab, however competent they might have been as political managers.

But with the appearance of television, to be successful, political leaders have had to demonstrate at least a minimum degree of "stage presence" in addition to their political skills, and their party's general acceptability on the basis of traditional support and position on contemporary issues. At the very least, they have had to be seen as being no less dynamic than their major opponents, lest they risk becoming liabilities to their party's electoral fortunes.

In this respect, one could argue that had Lester Pearson been able to project the kind of fervor that John Diefenbaker could through the medium of television, he might have led his party to majority victories rather than minority governments in 1963 or 1965. Similarly, the narrow election defeat of the Progressive Conservatives in 1972, which allowed the Liberals to cling precariously to power with a minority government, could be attributed at least in part to the image and style problems of Robert Stanfield; it is important to remember that no charges of incompetence, or intellectual or character weakness were ever laid against Mr. Stanfield. He was, in fact, highly respected, but simply considered uninspiring by those who observed his media performances.

His unfavorable media image — and in this case the contention broadly held is that it was unearned — had to do with the well-known incident of his fumbling a football during the 1974 campaign. Stanfield's reflections on this incident reveal commonly held perceptions about the role media play with respect to image politics:

> I look back on my own football incident. I didn't like it, but I'm glad it
> happened because it showed that I was not entirely responsible for my lack
> of success. I do not think for a moment that it caused us to lose the
> election. I don't want to make too much of it, but I do say that the reason
> the *Globe and Mail*, and other papers across the country, planked that on
> the front page was because they were engaging in image politics.[4]

Despite this, it is somewhat surprising that image was apparently not uppermost in the minds of those who chose Stanfield's successor. While Joe Clark did lead his party to a minority victory in 1979, the fact that his personal popularity was significantly less than that of Pierre Trudeau may well have prevented the victory from being more decisive. His brief period in office as prime minister apparently did little to enhance his personal stature, and Trudeau, having announced retirement, nonetheless remained to lend his sometimes cantankerous, but never uninteresting, presence to the Canadian political scene. The conclusion seems inescapable: the ability of a party leader to project himself is of crucial significance in political contests, although leadership alone, plainly, will not determine the outcome of elections.

It is not clear whether the focus on leadership currently characteristic of Canadian campaigns is a result of American influence or simply due to the nature of television itself. Marshall McLuhan, among other students of communication, has pointed out that dramatizing all news events, including electoral campaigns, is most easily accomplished by concentrating on personalities.[5] Nonetheless, the Canadian political system results in the election of a prime minister along with a number of other high-profile politicians. There is certainly ample opportunity for television to indulge its penchant for personalities by devoting greater coverage to these regional lieutenants and party heavyweights. It could be argued, for instance, that John Crosbie, Minister of Finance during the short-lived Tory government of 1979, would have been at least as interesting and dramatic a personage to feature in election coverage as was Joe Clark. Crosbie himself noted in a seminar on the media, however, that national television news preferred to cover his leader getting a haircut in Vancouver, rather than a major speech the minister was delivering in Toronto.[6]

It is not the media that totally determine this type of coverage. Leading political figures have an intense interest in gaining exposure. Thus Canadian politicians have fuelled this process by studying and emulating American-style campaigns. There are times when one wonders if Joe McGuinniss's *The Selling of the President*[7] has not become the handbook for Canadian party professionals. This has been done in full knowledge that television is only too willing to act in collusion with them in portraying Canadian national elections more and more as referenda on party leaders.

Campaign Negativism

The contest aura that is produced by this trend, the horserace coverage that was referred to earlier, has also led to the portrayal of electoral campaigns in an inordinately negative manner. This phenomenon is evident not only in the election news reporting that we examined in Chapters 3 and 4, but also in paid political advertisements sponsored by the political parties. The self-adopted role of critic is not new for the media: it has a long and honored tradition in the printed press. But again, the strength of television in dramatizing political events has emphasized the naturally confrontational elements of electioneering. In effect, we can recognize quite clearly that, like any news reporting, election coverage is a selection process. All the events in the day of a politician cannot be recorded; indeed if they were, most would be extremely dull. Therefore, what is dramatic, what stands out for attention, is what the media cover. And leaders tend to be dramatic in themselves.

We would not dispute that leaders are important. Certainly the capacity of a person to handle whatever unforeseen issues might face the country two or three years after the election is an appropriate concern for the thinking voter. However, positions and arguments on the contemporary issues are also important criteria for electoral decisions. The electorate needs to know what solutions are proposed for societal problems, how much they are going to cost, how they are going to be paid for, and what are likely to be their consequences. It would seem, therefore, that there is a place in election reporting for the careful unravelling of party policy by party leaders, and indeed by others in the party who may be more expert in the specifics of certain policies than the leader is. The confrontational style of reporting has detracted from this sorely needed type of party policy analysis. The newspaper, which has the space to devote to more intensive and reflective analysis of issues, has maintained its tradition of doing so, although the tabloid sector of the industry has led a trend away from serious reporting. Under the influence of television reporting, newspaper copy has tended to fall into the more negative confrontational framework as well. Writing of the 1979 election, Clive Cocking has argued that ''There has probably never been a Canadian election conducted in such an overwhelmingly negative atmosphere.''[8]

In the electronic media, news reporting of any sort tends to be very limited in length, given that individual items are included in tandem with perhaps a dozen to fifteen different stories in a 20-minute newscast. Unless a story is so highly unusual as to dominate a newscast, it is unlikely, even during an election campaign, for it to be longer than one or two minutes in length. A three-minute story is unusual. The norm is likely to be 20 to 40 seconds. An in-depth analysis of any serious political utterance is highly unlikely in such a short time span. Rather, the reporter tends to look for what stands out, what particular differs from the rest of the context, and, often, what lends itself to visual presentation (in the case of television). The practising politician must view the electoral process as a competition with opposing parties as well as their ideas, but the competitive elements attract more attention than the substantive issues. There is little doubt that reporters, searching for an attention-getting story for their editors, respond more favorably to the dramatic elements of the electoral process than they do to the hum-drum of fact-oriented debate. Indeed some reporters, persuaded that controversy is the ''stuff'' of news, are not above igniting controversies by the use of leading or provocative questioning. Attack and counter-attack dominate the reporting of elections and create a negative aura.

In fairness, it must be added that not all of today's journalism falls into such a confrontational style of reporting. Analyses of issues were made by broadcasters, particularly by CBC staffs during recent elections, and perhaps even more issue-oriented coverage may be evident in the future.

Nevertheless, the effects of this negativism extend beyond the campaign period itself. Having been fed a steady diet of reports of politicians' attacks on each other, reinforced by political columnists as well as advertising, it would be surprising indeed if Canadians didn't hold politicians and the political institutions they run in relatively low esteem.[9]

In a democratic society a healthy scepticism about power and those who wield it is a useful tool for maintaining a responsive government. However, when those who occupy decision-making positions are constantly portrayed as lacking in both morality and intelligence, the legitimacy of the decisions taken by the government may soon be called into question and the stability of the political system itself may be jeopardized. Unfortunately there is no calculus to determine the proper balance between responsible criticism of public figures to keep them on the straight and narrow, and according them and the institutions they represent enough respect so that they can carry out the public policy roles assigned to them. The media may have contributed to bringing the political system into a state of disrepute. If that reputation is deserved, the media have done a good job. If however, our political institutions are reasonably serviceable, the media have done something for which they must be held accountable.[10]

In many instances, there is no question that the disrepute surrounding politics and politicians is well deserved. We certainly believe it to be true, as media defenders frequently claim, that media do not manufacture news events, at least that the practice is rare and unusual and professional practitioners disavow the practice.[11] For example, Watergate and the immediate events surrounding Watergate were not media inventions. It is clear, however, that events of much less significance occasionally become colored and shaped by media as they are handled by inexperienced, sensation-seeking or unprofessional journalists looking to uncover their own Watergate. Politicians' human failings become amplified by such unprofessionalism, although their misdemeanors are magnified because they are performed by individuals who sought and then violated the public trust.

As mentioned in passing above, it is not only campaign news that has been framed in a negative cast: political advertising has also moved in the same direction. We have probably seen the last of ''The Land Is Strong'' genre ads as used by the Liberal Party in the 1972 campaign. More likely the message aimed at us, if present campaign styles persist, is ''The land will collapse if you elect those turkeys in the other parties.'' Parties, following the direction of their advertising agencies, have adopted the view that the destruction of their opponent's credibility is the most useful approach.

Jerry Grafstein, the Liberal Party advertising advisor, has said, ''Let's talk about the truth. Lawyers are never interested in asking whether a person is guilty or not. They just want to show that the other side can't prove that you're guilty or not, and that's what politics, in my view is all about.''[12] Political philosophers, with the possible exception of Machiavelli, would not be amused. Advertising strategies have replaced party platforms as the most important aspect of an appeal to the public.

Clive Cocking, reporting on Progressive Conservative advertising says, "As part of the planned strategy, the initial Tory commercials focused exclusively on Trudeau's failings, attempting to erode his leadership credibility."[13]

There is considerable debate about the impact of advertising.[14] Political parties, however, are convinced they must do a lot of it. The compacted period, and thus the hectic pace, of an election campaign creates a psychology that encourages a belief in the need to do at least as much advertising as the other side is doing. Unfortunately, short commercials are not tailored to the presentation of policy alternatives, but are rather more easily fashioned into vehicles for attack. This form of campaigning, like much else, is directed toward the more uncommitted and probably more disinterested voter. As such, political advertising is not aimed at swelling the ranks of the knowledgeable and interested voters. Rather it is crafted to make a transitory impact on the marginal ones.[15]

Of all creatures, politicians live most in the short term, their horizon being defined by the date of the next election. It takes an extraordinarily altruistic politician to willingly risk losing an election in order to benefit society as a whole in some future era. It just isn't easy to take the high ethical campaign road, when it is demonstrable that the low road leads to victory.

The negativism that has surrounded electoral campaigns in the 1970s and 1980s tends to obscure the major underlying reality about elections. That they take place at all and offer real choices to the electorate in terms of people and policy is fundamental to the democratic process. Detractors of the present social order argue that the choices take place in such a narrow spectrum of ideology that they are only confirmations of the status quo. Nonetheless those who feel they benefit from the present system (whether or not they are correct in this assessment) are in the majority. The differences between elections in Canada and those in one-party states, or where elections are skipped entirely, is the difference between a country where a wide degree of liberty exists and those where it is a scarce commodity. It is therefore important in Canada not to demean the electoral process. Electoral periods are a reconfirmation of those most basic elements of a democratic political system. It is important for the media to do more than make a ritualistic appeal for people to get out and vote on election day. They should also remind citizens that the importance of the event is more fundamental than the personalities and issues that dominate any particular election.

Public Opinion Polls and Electoral Campaigns

Another facet of modern electoral contests that has helped to crowd the serious discussion of issues from centre stage is the practice of public opinion polling. This provides ample fodder for the horserace style of political reporting. Indeed, as we pointed out in Chapters 3 and 4, polling was the fourth most mentioned theme in the electronic media coverage of the 1980 election, and ranked in ninth place in press coverage of the 1979 campaign. From the point of view of media behavior, the manner in which polling results should be transmitted to the public, or in fact if they should be published at all during the course of a campaign, are issues that have frequently been debated.

Although studies have indicated that polling does not alter the behavior of voters,[16] there are those who decry the potential influence of polls on the electoral process. One might suggest that the electoral law provision prohibiting the broadcast of election results while voting booths remain open could logically be extended to prohibiting publication of polling results during a campaign. Yet if there is that much concern about influencing the voters, should not politicians be precluded from arguing that the people are with them, or that public opinion is turning their way?

The real issue with regard to polls should be their reliability and how they are interpreted to the public by the news media. A properly conducted public opinion poll is a scientific attempt to discover one part of the truth surrounding an election: how people think about the various parties, leaders, and issues of the campaign. However, polls can be conducted on very slipshod bases, the most notorious (and unfortunately the most popular among media) being the "man on the street" interview. These "polls" are not serious attempts to arrive at the truth, and a reasonable argument for their suppression could be made. As well, political parties can engage in campaign strategies that involve the "leaking" of encouraging results from surveys that have been constructed to yield biased findings (the "dirty poll") at strategic points during the election.

The question with respect to polling is really one of ensuring that "scientific lies" are not presented by media in the guise of legitimate survey research. However, to argue that the results of legitimate and proper scientific inquiry should be suppressed is in fact to argue that some part of the truth should be kept from the public, a proposition that we reject. How society might monitor the quality of polling is not readily apparent, but it is not normally the practice in democratic society to prevent the publication of reliable information just to suppress unreliable data.

A related problem is the inability of many political journalists to interpret properly the results of polls or the statistical validity of their design. Even well-constructed polls with sample sizes in the neighborhood of 2,000 cannot claim absolute precision. The degree to which they may vary from certainty is known as the margin of error. Depending on the exact sample size, assuming that the random sample can be depended upon to be representative 95 out of 100 times, the margin of error might be as high as + or − 3% in the typical electoral campaign survey. As sample sizes decrease, the margin of error increases. If random sampling techniques were not used, it is impossible to calculate the margin of error. But only lip service is given in the media to the usual disclaimer about margins of error. For example, in a close election a poll might be reported as indicating that one party is slightly ahead. However, the margin of error may be such that, in fact, another party might well be in the lead.

Control of Communications:
The Federal/Provincial Controversy

The communications media in Canada operate within a political system in which almost everything of importance has come to involve federal-provincial relations. The media are interwoven into this process for they are crucial in disseminating information and opinions about federal-provincial relations. Moreover, control of the media themselves is an outstanding issue in the debate over the distribution of federal and provincial powers.

Formal constitutional power over the media has been vested in the federal government. For the first 50 years or so of Canada's constitutional history, this meant little since newspapers were unregulated and the broadcast media didn't exist. Time and technology have conspired to create a problem. The Fathers of Confederation assigned powers to federal and provincial domains and on that basis broadcasting was later judged to be under federal jurisdiction. Education, however, was from the beginning made the exclusive preserve of the provinces. Where then was the proper jurisdictional authority when educational broadcasting came into being? As a result of this ambiguity, in the modern era some provinces have demanded an expanded role in controlling the electronic media. The coming of cable enlarged this conflict. Quebec, with its traditional concern over control of those aspects of society that affect culture, has attempted to enter into the licensing field despite objections and stiff resistance of Ottawa. Saskatchewan has been a leader in the struggle for provincial control of cable, and even wants a role in licensing broadcasting outlets. The provincial ownership of telephone companies, which can act as carriers, lends technical credence to the demands of these provinces.

These concerns led to the inclusion of the area of communications as one of the items for debate during the 1980-81 discussions regarding the patriation of the constitution, an amendment process, a charter of rights, and changes in the division of powers between federal and provincial levels of government. While in the final analysis the first three were accomplished with a degree of compromise in the Canada Act of 1982, the question of control of communications is one of those areas of dispute that remains outstanding and must await future constitutional amendments.

The federal government has always seen communications as a vital instrument in fostering political integration. It has been willing to talk to the provinces about expanding their roles, but is reluctant to give up the dominant position Ottawa has occupied in this field from the beginning. Given the centrality of media to processes of nation-building, the spectre of ten provincially regulated media systems is enough to traumatize those Canadians who value the concept of a strongly integrated country.

To a degree provinces already have the capacity to affect the way the media report on elections. Each province, after all, has its own set of laws governing provincial elections. During the Quebec Referendum, in 1980, the Quebec government, which in no sense was a neutral observer of the event, was in a position to dictate through its legislative majority the rules that would govern the campaign. This, of course, included the amounts of advertising that could be undertaken by the opposing positions in the debate.

The Quebec Referendum had obvious national implications, but the federal government was not in a position to dictate the way in which media would be used for advertising purposes. On the contrary, we find the national radio and television services bound by journalistic norms that call for balanced reporting.[17] Here is a real paradox: a national broadcasting service, mandated legislatively to preserving national unity, giving equal coverage to a movement whose aim was the disintegration of the state. Yet it is possible those who felt that the French service had been heavily infiltrated by separatists viewed balanced treatment as an improvement over the favorable treatment of separatism, which federal Liberal politicians had accused the French service of disseminating.[18]

One of the results of this set of circumstances was the consternation created by the timing of an alcohol abuse campaign sponsored by the federal government, featuring the use of the word "NON" in large letters. Premier Lévesque saw in this a dastardly subterfuge to circumvent the Quebec Referendum rules. To those deeply involved in this process, it would have been easy to overlook the ironic elements involved in the referendum debate: the federal government was in a sense expected to "butt out" of a decision that would affect the very structure of the country it governed. Perhaps the net result of the conduct of the referendum was to demonstrate how committed to peace, order, and good government Canadians really are. Few, if any, debates over the dismantling of a country could have taken place in such a gentlemanly and non-violent context.

The Regulatory Dilemma

The role of government in the regulation of electronic mass media is becoming more and more problematic. Only a few years ago the Canadian Radio-television Commission and its predecessors carried on their regulatory work more comfortably, because there was a firm understanding about the basis of broadcasting. It was clear that the broadcasting spectrum had limitations in engineering terms, therefore, the airwaves were considered to be a "scarce resource" to be conserved. Moreover, broadcasting was not deemed to be an end in itself. Broadcasting was, as the regulators repeatedly pointed out, subject to higher imperatives of nation-building and cultural survival.

The resultant protectionism discussed in the previous chapter has had many dimensions. A list of these includes: the content quotas for broadcasting stations, whereby Canadian resources were to be harnessed in an effective manner so as to protect the integrity of the Canadian identity; the regulation of cable television systems by demanding a priority channel system for the distribution of Canadian signals rather than American signals; the deletion of US "lifestyle" television commercials in programs that flowed into Canada; the attempts to control, by licensing, the importation of non-Canadian television materials through satellite transmission systems; the attempts to de-commercialize the CBC's operations so that the corporation could function as a central nervous system to a Canadian broadcasting industry that lacked a sharp direction in terms of the industry's mandate; the variety of tax incentive measures to keep Canadian advertising dollars within the country; and the imposition of a Canadian content quota system for magazines published in Canada so that they might qualify as "Canadian" in terms of accepting Canadian advertisements.

To what extent such protectionism has been effective is questionable. Using the yardstick of Canadian unity, one must concede that a strong political national cohesiveness is absent and that regional loyalties remain strong. National broadcasting and other Ottawa-generated forces simply have not been powerful enough to overcome regional differences and geographical distances, and provincial demands for territorial prerogatives have strengthened and increased.

With regard to television, the medium with the largest impact, when given a choice, the English-speaking Canadian public continues to express a preference for American content. At least this is true of entertainment, if much less so in terms of news broadcasting. Indeed the Canadian Broadcasting Corporation by the scheduling of popular US television programming into its own prime time broadcasting, has done little to discourage Canadians from viewing lifestyle content from a foreign society. Satellite dishes that are capable of bringing foreign content into homes are becoming increasingly popular in Canada. Attempts by federal authorities to regulate these were abandoned in early 1983.[19] Further, the ready availability of popular non-Canadian entertainment through home video recorder-playback units, and the introduction of Pay-TV in Canada, all cater to the entertainment preferences of Canadian audiences — and these preferences tend not to be for Canadian materials.

The extent to which the CRTC protectionist policies can effectively foster Canadian identity is at the moment in doubt. For example, in a March 1983 announcement with respect to developing broadcasting technologies, federal Communications Minister Francis Fox announced, among other new policies, that individual Canadians would no longer require licences for privately owned satellite receiving antennas. This policy change was based on the inability of federal authorities to regulate the spread of the use of such antennas and the difficulty and failure to prosecute those who, despite government prohibitions, adopted their use for the importation of non-Canadian programming. The present situation, which is unlikely to change in the short run, is that the tastes and preferences of Canadian television viewers are satisfied by foreign ideas and materials, despite whatever urgency Ottawa authorities may express about the need to encourage the selection of domestic content.

Advocacy Advertising

Advocacy advertising began to receive broad public attention in the early 1970s because of the now-celebrated effort by Mobil Oil in the United States to put its case regarding the benefits of offshore drilling before the American public.[20] Two of the three major networks in the US — CBS and ABC — refused to carry Mobil's message. These refusals were interpreted by Mobil as a denial of the public's right to have important information and as a restraint on free, open discussion of matters of public interest.

In Canada, three different studies of advocacy advertising have taken place, and each has managed to shed light on this new style of communication.

First, in the spring of 1977, a meeting was convened by the Canadian Bar Association, the Faculty of Law at the University of Toronto, and the Task Force on Freedom of Broadcasting Information, Canadian Radio-television Commission. There, a definition of advocacy advertising was offered by a representative of the Association of Canadian Advertisers:

> Advocacy advertising is something more than advertising directed to improve a corporate image; it attempts to inform and persuade the public about matters that are not directly related to the sale of a product or a service. It reacts and retaliates against unfair attacks upon such of the free enterprise system as remains. It attempts to influence government and the public at election time.[21]

Second, in November 1981, the Public Affairs Division of the Conference Board of Canada held a conference on advocacy advertising. The Conference Board described advocacy advertising as a means of communication that "business, government and special interest groups have recently adopted to place their message directly before the public without intermediary interpretation by the press or others not disposed to their viewpoint."[22]

Finally, the Ontario Educational Communication Authority in February 1982 broadcast a four-part series of televised discussions on advertising. Two of the half-hour programs were devoted to advocacy advertising. In one of these telecasts, a representative from a major business firm in the United States observed that there was a particular need for advocacy advertising and that, in its origins, it was a presentation of information on the back pages of newspapers to correct impressions made by journalists on the front pages.[23]

Advocacy advertising is point-of-view advertising of a controversial social or political nature, which has as its purpose the changing of official policy in a society. It is a relatively new phenomenon on the mass media scene, but the debate about advocacy advertising is, in fact, another facet of the debate about freedom of expression in open societies.

For example, advocacy advertising is clearly a reaction against the inability — or unwillingness — of mass media to provide for adequate expression of major social and political points of view. The problem, however, is that in order to participate as an advocate about a major point of view, one must first be able to afford to purchase advertising. While the Canadian Broadcasting Corporation has been hesitatant about accepting advertising of a controversial or opinionated sort,[24] several Canadian newspapers openly invite firms and organizations to buy space to express points of view.

The matter takes on paramount importance in an open society where the government uses advertising to advocate its own points of view. In Canada, it is particularly noteworthy that the federal government, in a matter of a few years, has become by far the largest advertising account in the country. Provincial governments have hefty advertising budgets as well. The situation becomes immensely grating for opposition parties, who perceive that such advertising has usurped the traditional role of debate in Parliament, as well as providing the government party an almost unlimited budget to present its point of view. This, they argue, is a gross misuse of taxpayers' money. While they have been successful in raising the issue to some degree of public prominence, they have not been able to curb the growth of the practice.

Insofar as the central matter of this book is concerned, it must be observed here that a new political role for mass media has emerged. Because this country's mass media (with the qualified exception of the government-subsidized CBC) depend upon advertising for their revenues and their existence, political points of view are now being promoted — not debated — in a manner similar to competing commercial products. One might well speculate on the extent to which advocacy advertising could alter and perhaps subvert the political democratic process.

It is clear, of course, that advocacy advertising, in somewhat different formats, has been with us for many years. Government agencies have, in fact, been involved in the creation of a public consensus on the fundamental principles by which they are governed. However, in the light of massive advertising campaigns already experienced by Canadian society with respect to the Quebec Referendum of 1980 and the constitutional debates of 1981, it becomes conceivable that the government, given the vast financial resources available to it, could orchestrate persuasive informational campaigns in its own political interest against which society could well become defenceless.

Political Integration

The role of the media in fostering political integration, national unity as it is most often described in Canada, has been a recurrent theme in this and other books dealing with communications in this country. Political integration has been more or less accepted unquestioningly as a desirable end by the majority of Canadians outside the ranks of those Quebeckers who seek an independent status for their province. Unfortunately, desirable goals don't always dovetail perfectly and in this case the communications media also have legitimate concerns for other objectives (freedom of the press, for example), whose pursuit may not always foster national unity. Indeed, freedom of expression and expecting national unity as a consequence of media behavior may be mutually exclusive concepts. It is entirely possible that, if media were to be conscripted for nation-building efforts, Canadians would have to be prepared to accept a significant erosion of their current rights to freedom of expression.

The most difficult conflict arises from the responsibility to report events as they occur, including any serious disruptions that may threaten national political integration. The media cannot ignore an episode like the air traffic controllers' strike of 1976, much less the election of a Parti Québecois government.[25] Yet the amount of coverage given this kind of story, as well as the manner in which they are treated, can serve to direct public opinion in one direction or another and possibly make political accommodations more difficult. The tendency to underline the confrontational aspects of these developments invites the public to take sides with the combatants rather than reflect that each "side" has legitimate interests to protect and good arguments to make. The compromise that must ultimately be the outcome of most of these disagreements is not fostered by such a style of reporting. The characterization of major problems as personal confrontations — Trudeau versus Lougheed or Trudeau versus Lévesque — further trivializes fundamental structural problems of the Canadian federation and adds nothing to a search for their solution.

As always, politicians are not blameless in this situation. They are quick to seize upon this style of reporting as an instrument for short-term political gain. Provincial leaders bash the federal government as an important element in their election campaigns, with the sure knowledge that the media will be only too ready to give coverage to their aggressive posture and transmit it to their provincial electorate. This is especially effective with newspapers, which with few exceptions are aimed at a local audience.

This last point indicates another factor that may make the media run counter to their mandate (certainly the electronic media mandate) to promote national unity. Provincial or regional reporting emphasis may deny to the public a more Canada-wide view of the problems facing the national polity. This is especially true of the francophone media of Quebec. From what we can gather, however, it is less true during national election campaigns than during normal times. By their very nature, national elections induce even the francophone press to create an agenda that approximates the English one, thereby creating a national agenda.

The Toronto- and Montreal-centred concentration of the communications media in Canada could, it would seem, provide a focus for national integration. That factor in itself, however, generates some hostility in the western and eastern regions of the country. The tendency to view what is happening in those two major cities, and of course in Ottawa, as representative of the national scene signals to other parts of the country an ignorance of and insensitivity to the needs and opinions of anyone outside of central Canada. Here we again run into the basic structural reality of Canada and its inherent problems.

One-fourth of Canada's population lives in the metropolitan areas of

Toronto and Montreal. Within just 400 km of each of those cities lives over half of the Canadian population. In this area one finds not just the communications centre of Canada, but also its national capital, its financial centre, and most of its industrial capacity. The view that most of what is important in Canada is happening in this area is all too easy to accept and it seems that many journalists fall victim to it. That only serves to underline the frustration of people in Vancouver, Edmonton, or Halifax, who sometimes feel that they are considered poor (and dull) country cousins, hardly worth mentioning in the national news or in central Canadian newspapers. The stridency of Albertans, after the oil boom, is to some degree an announcement to Toronto and Montreal pundits that they would have to pay attention to the west from now on. Their complaints about too much attention being given to Quebec is another way of saying that the west's problems are just as important and warrant equal or similar national attention.

How is it possible to cater to the needs of the majority of the population concentrated in the Quebec City–Windsor corridor, while at the same time paying proper attention to other areas of Canada where the population is smaller and more dispersed? There is no easy answer. The concentration of important news communication facilities and personnel in New York has not created a problem of the same magnitude in the United States. While there may be some resentment in the hinterland, the degree of American political integration is such that the situation is not held up as an example of some flaw in the system. In Canada, however, it does rankle many that a Toronto newspaper styles itself "Canada's National Newspaper" or that the CBC news program, "The National" is broadcast only from Toronto. Relocation of central facilities is not an easy solution. Greater sensitivity to the problems and attitudes of Canadians outside of Ontario and Quebec, however, may provide a basis for a more solid contribution of the media to political integration.

There is of course a difference in the capacity of the print and electronic media to contribute to political integration. A radio or television news program can be heard simultaneously across Canada, or arranged to be on at the same hour in different time zones. Newspapers, however, are by their nature more localized.[26] It is true that the Canadian Press distributes items by wire to newspapers in different locations in the country and there is also an array of syndicated columnists who appear in a number of newspapers. This does help give a national tone to the news, but it does not eliminate the varying importance of certain items in one region of the country as opposed to another. The newspaper chains argue strenuously that rather than exercising tight control, which could perhaps foster a national outlook, they afford complete editorial freedom to the publishers of individual papers. This permits the development of their localized interests, supported by the financial resources of a large and, as they would have us believe, a benign corporation, dedicated to the freedom of the press and the odd dollar in profit, if that is possible.

In Canada the magazine industry hasn't developed in a way that would provide a print medium that is more national in scope. Until it was made unwelcome in Canada through the federal government's exercise of power through the tax laws, *Time*, which had a small Canadian section, was the most widely circulated news magazine. What bigger irony could there have been than for an essentially American magazine to have been expected to exercise a role in fostering Canadian unity? Of course it accepted no such mandate. Other magazines did exist, such as *Maclean's, Saturday Night,* and *Canadian Forum*, but these did not compete in circulation. The latter two were more limited in their appeal in any case and even for their more restricted readership, could make little claim to being agencies of political integration between the regions and linguistic groups of Canada. The restrictions imposed on *Time* have given *Maclean's* the opportunity to adopt a more vital role in national integration, but whether that will transpire is still to be determined. *Maclean's* is also dominated by the eastern communications establishment.

What is not subject to speculation is the fact that for most of their history Canadians have read more American magazines than those published in Canada.[27] The magazine, a print medium that could have fostered Canadian political integration, simply was not developed because of American penetration.

That penetration has been curbed somewhat, allowing the magazine industry in Canada to make some large strides forward. Whether that industry will be part of a future process of greater national integration may be questionable, but there is no doubt of its unsuccessful past.

Conclusions

The argument that the media ought to make a contribution to political integration in Canada usually presupposes that political integration is a good thing. Quebec separatists, to name the most obvious dissenters, would not accept that, or at least they would be more concerned with political integration within Quebec. Political integration is not the only goal of a state like Canada. The pursuit of social order and democratic practices, the exercise of individual rights, and the attainment of economic prosperity are all aims of the political system in Canada. What role will the media play in supporting the political system's attempts to maintain itself and to pursue these goals? Certainly this role is important during an election that itself is an event of intrinsic importance in confirming the democratic nature of Canada as well as determining who will govern.

Our findings indicate that the media for the most part constitute a supporting structure for the political system in Canada. The fundamental tenets of government are not challenged by the media, either during election periods or outside them. By presenting the Canadian community with a relatively common agenda of the problems facing them, the media reinforce the reality of a political entity known as Canada. No doubt different regions, linguistic groups, and interest groups view from differing perspectives the solutions being put forward by contestants for their votes. Nonetheless, that there is some common agreement on what it is that needs solving helps to confirm the Canadian political experience.

As noted above, the generally critical interpretation of politicians encourages public mistrust of them. This mistrust may affect the electorate's view of the system itself. However, to this point there has not been any general clamor for electoral reform, let alone more fundamental challenges to the established order. Overall, while one may criticize the media on several fronts, it could not be realistically argued that they are undermining the very existence of Canada. The media depiction of violence is cited by some as a factor in the deterioration of social order. Few, however, would argue that the media have a primary responsibility for that problem. On the other hand, a good case can be made that the media are leading agents in the struggle for the preservation and extension of democratic norms and individual rights.

In their seemingly unrelenting attacks on whoever is governing, at whatever level of government in Canada, the media create problems for many of those who lead Canada. For many leaders those problems are well deserved. The question is one of finding the proper balance between legitimate criticism and deserving praise. It would be unfair to the media to say that their performance is so miserable that they have made governing impossible in Canada, but it would not be unfair to say that the reporting and analysis modes adopted by the media have done little to encourage public respect for the people who direct our public affairs.

Those who work in the media have a crucial responsibility to the Canadian public. In carrying out that responsibility, media practitioners have been militant defenders of a free press as a bulwark of a healthy democratic society. Other Canadians have a right to expect more than just a defence of the media's right to pursue their work without interference; they have a right to expect the media to dedicate themselves to a greater degree of insight into their own roles and a more professional commitment to fulfilling their responsibility.

Notes

1W. C. Soderlund and R. H. Wagenberg, "A Content Analysis of Editorial Coverage of the 1972 Election Campaigns in Canada and the United States," *Western Political Quarterly*, XXVIII (March 1975), p. 91.

2The issue of the Americanization of Canadian politics is discussed by Denis Smith, "President and Parliament: The Transformation of Parliamentary Government in Canada," in Thomas A. Hockin, ed., *Apex of Power: Prime Minister and Political Leadership in Canada* (Toronto: Prentice-Hall, 1971), pp. 224-41. Smith argues that, among other factors, "if anything has accelerated the trend towards presidential politics in Canada it has been the enthusiastic adoption of televised leadership conventions" (p. 234).

3At a seminar that examined the political, economic, and cultural relationships between Canada and the United States, the following comment was made: "the fundamental similarity between our two countries which binds us even more intimately than the links of history, geography, economics and communications, is that we both bear allegiance to the 'democratic idea.''' In that fundamental link, the two nations share a common purpose in preserving "their ideals in a world convulsed by revolutionary changes." See J. Duncan Edmonds, "The Situation of Democracy in Canada and America," *Proceedings of the Fourth Seminar on Canadian-American Relations* (Windsor: Assumption University of Windsor, 1962), pp. 24-37.

At the same time, it has been a major concern of those who, historically, have been charged with the design of national policies for Canadian telecommunication systems to repel the advances of "continentalism," which arises from the abundance of interplay of forces between Canada and the United States. Such a threat has been described as the "strong north-south pull of continentalism" and as a "natural force of economic gravity which operates on north-south lines." See Communications Canada, *Proposal For a Communications Policy for Canada* (Ottawa: Information Canada, 1973), pp. 3, 5.

[4]Robert Stanfield, "Summing Up," in *Politics and the Media: An Examination of the Issues Raised by the Quebec Referendum and the 1979 and 1980 Federal Elections* (Toronto: Readers Digest Foundation, 1981), p. 120.

[5]Marshall McLuhan, *Understanding Media*, 2nd. ed. (New York: Signet Books, The New American Library, 1964), pp. 287-8.

[6]John Crosbie, "Politics and the Media: Is the Public Well Served?" in *Politics and the Media*, p. 10.

[7]Joe McGinniss, *The Selling of the President* (New York: Trident, 1969). Important also are Theodore White's series on American presidential campaigns, beginning with *The Making of the President 1960* (New York: Atheneum, 1961).

[8]Clive Cocking, *Following the Leaders: A Media Watcher's Diary of Campaign '79* (Toronto: Doubleday Canada, 1980), p. 280.

[9]See the *Globe and Mail*, January 27, 1983, p. 1. An article by Michael Keenan examines a poll conducted by the Centre for Applied Research in the Apostolate, in which a sample of 1200 Canadians of all religious persuasions were interviewed. Confidence in the civil service stood at 49%, the press at 44%, and Parliament at 42%. Frederick J. Fletcher and Robert J. Drummond report a general decline in the sense of political efficacy on the part of Canadians over the period 1965 to 1974. They also report a decrease in the level of trust in goverment, from 66% trusting the government to do what is right in 1968 to 57% feeling this way in 1977. The poll reported in the *Globe and Mail*, while somewhat differently worded, seems to indicate a further erosion of support for and trust in government. See F. J. Fletcher and R. J. Drummond, *Canadian Attitude Trends 1960-1978* (Montreal: Institute for Research on Public Policy, 1979), pp. 67-70.

[10]On this point see Anthony Westell, "The Press: Adversary or Channel of Communication?" in Harold D. Clarke, Colin Campbell, F. Q. Quo, and Arthur Goddard, eds., *Parliament, Policy, and Representation* (Toronto: Methuen, 1980), pp. 25-34.

[11]However, Edwin Black adopts the point of view that in some sense, all "news" is created by the media as a product of their production processes. See his chapter entitled "The Manufacture of News" in *Politics and the News* (Toronto:Butterworths, 1982).

[12]Jerry Grafstein, "The Anatomy of a Campaign. The Federal Election and the Referendum, or Who Manages Whom?" in *Politics and the Media*, p. 68.

[13]Cocking, p. 260.

[14]Research about advertising effects is normally conducted at three levels: first, at the individual, consumer response–behavioral level; second, at the message-market level; third, at the broad social level (advertising as an institution in society and the consequent effects on other social institutions). Two journals, in particular, focus attention on advertising research — the *Journal of Advertising Research* and the *Journal of Marketing Research*. For an overview of the three areas cited above, see S. Watson Dunn and Arnold M. Barban, *Advertising: Its Role in Modern Marketing*, 5th ed. (Toronto: Holt, Rinehart and Winston, 1982): pp. 66-103, 272-95.

[15]William O. Gilsdorf, "Getting the Message Across: The Communication Strategy of the Federal Liberal Party in the 1979 and 1980 Canadian Federal Elections." Paper presented to the Annual Meeting of the Canadian Communication Association, Université du Québec à Montréal, 1980, pp. 43-6.

[16]Bernard Hennessy, *Public Opinion*, 4th ed. (Monterey, Calif.: Brooks/Cole Publishing, 1981), pp. 92-3; with respect to Canada see Frederick J. Fletcher, *The Newspaper and Public Affairs*, Vol. 7, Research Publications, Royal Commission on Newspapers (Ottawa: Ministry of Supply and Services Canada, 1981), p. 91. On the other hand, Flora Lewis has argued that in recent European elections, polls have allowed voters to assess the relative strength of parties and to react accordingly in order to send finely tuned messages to their political leaders. Without proportional representation, however, the Canadian system does not easily afford this opportunity. Nevertheless, it is certainly possible to see polls as a positive influence on the democratic process as well as a negative one. See Flora Lewis, "Polls finally benefit voters," the Windsor *Star*, March 21, 1983, p. A-10.

[17]For an analysis of media coverage of the Quebec Referendum, see Peter Halford, Adrien van den Hoven, W. C. Soderlund, and W. I. Romanow, "A Media Tale of Two Cities: Media Coverage of the Quebec Referendum in Montreal and Toronto," *Canadian Journal of Communication* 9 (Autumn 1983), 1-31.

[18]See CRTC, *Report by the Committee of Inquiry into the National Broadcasting Service* (Ottawa, July 20, 1977), pp. 35-6 for details on perceived biases in the CBC network.

[19]See John Gray, "More U.S. Shows, Satellite TV Dishes get Ottawa's Nod," the *Globe and Mail*, March 2, 1983, pp. 1-2.

[20]For a detailed discussion and reproduction of Mobil Oil's subsequent newspaper advertisements, see Dunn and Barban, pp. 366-70.

[21]*Seminar: Advocacy Advertising*, Leslie Wallace, transcript editor, (Ottawa: CRTC, 1977), p. 16.

[22]*Advocacy Advertising: Propaganda or Democratic Right? A Report From the Public Affairs Research Division of the Conference Board of Canada*, Duncan McDowell, ed. (Ottawa: The Conference Board of Canada, 1982), p. vii.

[23]Ontario Educational Communications Authority (TV Ontario), four telecasts entitled "Quartets: Advertising," February, 1982.

[24]*Seminar: Advocacy Advertising*, pp. 17-8.

[25]W. C. Soderlund, R. H. Wagenberg, R. C. Nelson, and E. D. Briggs, "Regional and Linguistic Agenda Setting in Canada: A Study of Newspaper Coverage of Issues Affecting Political Integration in 1976," *Canadian Journal of Political Science*, XIII (June 1980), pp. 347-56.

[26]In a national study performed by the Communications Research Centre in

Toronto for the Royal Commission on Newspapers (1981), Canadians were invited to respond to a question about which of the three media—radio, television, or newspapers—they would choose for keeping best informed about "what happens in your area." Responses were as follows: newspapers 59%; radio 25%; television 18%. On the other hand, when asked the same question with respect to world and international news, Canadians responded in this manner: television 55%; newspapers 30%; radio 24%. See Leonard Kubas with the Communications Research Centre, *Newspapers and Their Readers, Volume I: Research Publications Report of the Royal Commission on Newspapers* (Ottawa: Ministry of Supply and Services Canada, 1981), p. 26. Such emphasis on newspapers for local information has also been true with respect to electioneering. Results of research in the US confirm that "when people think 'local' politics, they tend to think 'newspapers'; when they think 'state' or 'national' politics, they tend to think 'television.'" See Burns W. Roper, *An Extended View of Public Attitudes Toward Television and Other Mass Media 1959-1971* (New York: Television Information Office, 1971), p. 9.

[27]*The Uncertain Mirror: Report of the Special Senate Committee on Mass Media,* Volume I (Ottawa: Information Canada, 1970), p. 156. See also Frederick J. Fletcher and Daphne F. Gottleib, "The Mass Media and the Political Process," in Michael Whittington and Glen Williams, eds., *Canadian Politics in the 1980's* (Toronto: Methuen, 1981), p. 146.

Appendix

CONTENT ANALYSIS EXERCISE

Since this book will be used more frequently in periods where there is no election taking place than during election campaigns, we decided to include a more general exercise in content analysis rather than one that focuses specifically on elections. We would hope that this exercise, or modifications of it, might be incorporated as a practical exercise in courses in which this book is used.

For this particular exercise, two or more newspapers are required. We would suggest a period of study of two weeks at minimum, more preferably three or four weeks. During this period, each daily issue of the newspaper should be analyzed. Of course, either a random sample or an every two or three day sample could be used.

We would suggest examining front page news stories and editorials only. The following variables can be coded:

AREA OF FOCUS OF
STORY/EDITORIAL
1. international
2. national
3. provincial
4. local
5. human interest
6. other (specify)

PLACEMENT OF
STORY/EDITORIAL
1. Lead story/editorial
2. non-lead story/editorial

TYPE OF STORY
1. just text, no photo, etc,
2. text accompanied by photo, chart, map, etc.
3. just photo, chart, map etc. with no text other than caption
4. other (specify)
5. non-applicable

SOURCE OF STORY
1. local staff (by-lined story by a reporter affiliated with the paper)
2. Canadian Press (CP)
3. other Canadian sources
4. American Wire Services
5. European Wire Services
6. other
7. unknown/non-applicable

For editorials, code only AREA OF FOCUS and PLACEMENT variables.

For each front page story and editorial, use a copy of the code sheet reproduced on the opposite page and check the appropriate categories.

Percentages of each category, for each variable, for each newspaper can either be computed manually by the student, or the data can easily be put into an SPSS data set for computer analysis.

For more detailed information on content analysis in general and on intercoder reliability especially, we direct the student to Ole Holsti, *Content Analysis for Social Sciences and Humanities* (Reading, Mass.: Addison-Wesley, 1969).

CONTENT ANALYSIS EXERCISE
CODE SHEET

NEWSPAPER			DATE	
LANGUAGE	FRENCH	OWNERSHIP	SOUTHAM	
	ENGLISH		THOMSON	
PROVINCE	NEWFOUNDLAND		IRVING	
	PEI		ARMADALE	
	NOVA SCOTIA		SIFTON	
	NEW BRUNSWICK		GESCA	
	QUEBEC		UNIMEDIA	
	ONTARIO		QUEBECOR	
	MANITOBA		INDEPENDENT	
	SASKATCHEWAN		OTHER	
	ALBERTA	TYPE OF CONTENT	FRONT PAGE	
	BC		EDITORIAL	
AREA OF FOCUS OF STORY	INTERNATIONAL	PLACEMENT OF STORY	LEAD	
	NATIONAL		NON-LEAD	
	PROVINCIAL	SOURCE OF STORY	LOCAL STAFF (by-lined story by a reporter affiliated with the newspaper)	
	LOCAL			
	HUMAN INTEREST			
	OTHER			
TYPE OF STORY	JUST TEXT (no photo, etc.)		CANADIAN PRESS	
	TEXT ACCOMPANIED BY PHOTO ETC.		OTHER CANADIAN SOURCES	
			AMERICAN WIRE SERVICES	
	JUST PHOTO, CHART, MAP (no text other than caption)		EUROPEAN WIRE SERVICES	
			OTHER	
	OTHER		UNKNOWN/NON-APPLICABLE	
	NON-APPLICABLE			

Bibliography

BERELSON, Bernard R., Paul F. LAZARSFELD, and Hazel GAUDET. *The People's Choice*. New York: Columbia University Press, 1944.

BERELSON, Bernard R., Paul F. LAZARSFELD, and William N. MCPHEE. *Voting*. Chicago: University of Chicago Press, 1954.

BISHOP, Lee, Robert MEADOW, and Marilyn JOHNSON-BECK, editors. *The Presidential Debates: Media, Electoral, and Policy Perspectives*. New York: Praeger, 1978.

BLACK, Edwin R. *Politics and the News*. Toronto: Butterworth's, 1982.

BLACK, Edwin R. and Alan C. CAIRNS. "A Different Perspective on Canadian Federalism" *Canadian Public Administration*, 9 (1966), 27-44.

BLUMLER, Jay G. "The Role of Theory in Uses and Gratifications Studies" *Communication Research*, 6 (1979), 9-36.

BOOTH, Alan. "The Recall of News Items" *Public Opinion Quarterly*, 34 (1970-71), 604-10.

BOYLE, Harry J. Address to the Second National Conference of Journalists, Ottawa, 11 March 1972.

BROADBENT, Edward. "On Independence and Socialism" *Canadian Forum*, 52 (1972), p. 31.

CAMPBELL, Angus, et.al. *The American Voter*. New York: John Wiley & Sons, 1960.

———. *Elections and the Political Order*. New York: John Wiley & Sons, 1966.

CANADA. *Report of the Royal Commission on Radio Broadcasting, 1929*. Ottawa: The King's Printer, 1929.

———. *Debates of the House of Commons*. Seventeenth Parliament, Volume 3, May 18, 1932. Ottawa: The King's Printer, 1932.

———. *A Statement of Policy of the Canadian Broadcasting Corporation with Respect to Controversial Broadcasting*. Ottawa: Canadian Broadcasting Corporation, 1939.

———. *Political and Controversial Broadcasting: Policies and Rulings*. Ottawa: Canadian Broadcasting Corporation, 1948.

———. *Report of the Royal Commission on National Development in the Arts, Letters and Sciences, 1949-1951*. Ottawa: The King's Printer, 1951.

———. *Report of the Royal Commission on Broadcasting*. Ottawa: The Queen's Printer, 1957.

———. *Canadian Broadcasting Act*. Ottawa: The Queen's Printer, 1958.

———. *Announcement Regarding Radio (TV) Broadcast Regulations*. Ottawa: Board of Broadcast Governors, Nov. 18, 1959.

———. *Proposed Television Broadcasting Station Regulations*. Ottawa: Board of Broadcast Governors, July 28, 1959.

———. *Report of the Royal Commission on Publication*. Ottawa: The Queen's Printer, 1961.

———. *White Paper on Political and Controversial Broadcasting Policies*. Ottawa: Board of Broadcast Governors, Dec. 18, 1961.

———. *Proposals for a Communications Policy for Canada.* Ottawa: Information Canada, 1963.

———. *Report of the Committee on Broadcasting, 1965.* Ottawa: The Queen's Printer, 1965.

———. *White Paper on Broadcasting, 1966.* Ottawa: The Queen's Printer, 1966.

———. *Report on the White Paper on Broadcasting 1966.* House of Commons Standing Committee on Broadcasting, Films and Assistance to the Arts. Ottawa: The Queen's Printer, 1967.

———. *Broadcasting Act of 1968.* Ottawa: Queen's Printer, 1968.

———. *Broadcasters as Political Candidates.* (Announcement) Ottawa: Canadian Radio-television Commission, May 24, 1968.

———. *Direction to the Radio-television Commission Pursuant to Section 27 of the Broadcasting Act, P.C. 1969-2229.* Ottawa: The Queen's Printer, 1969.

———. *The Improvement and Development of Canadian Broadcasting and the Extension of U.S. Television Coverage in Canada by CATV.* Ottawa: Canadian Radio-television Commission, 1969.

———. *Report of the Senate Committee on Mass Media: Volume I, The Uncertain Mirror.* Ottawa: The Queen's Printer, 1970.

———. *Television Programs.* Press release. Ottawa: Canadian Radio-television Commission, Feb. 12, 1970.

———. *Report of the Special Senate Committee on Mass Media: Volume II, Words, Music and Dollars.* Ottawa: Information Canada, 1970.

———. *Excerpts from the Report of the Special Committee on "Air of Death."* Ottawa: Canadian Radio-television Commission, July 9, 1970.

———. *Annual Report.* Ottawa: Canadian Radio-television Commission, 1970, 1971.

———. *Canadian Broadcasting: "A Single System": Policy Statement on Cable Television.* Ottawa: Canadian Radio-television Commission, July 16, 1971.

———. *Broadcasters as Political Candidates* (announcement) Ottawa: Canadian Radio-television Commission, July 17, 1972.

———. *CRTC Facts Digest on Broadcasting and Telecommunications in Canada.* Ottawa: CRTC, 1972.

———. *Proposal for a Communications Policy for Canada.* Ottawa: Information Canada, 1973.

———. *The Canadian Broadcasting Corporation: A Brief History.* Ottawa: Canadian Broadcasting Corporation, 1976.

———. *Royal Commission on Corporate Concentration: Study Number 23, The Newspaper Firm and Freedom of Information.* Ottawa: Supply and Services, 1977.

———. *Report of the Committee of Inquiry into the National Broadcasting Service.* Ottawa: Canadian Radio-television Commission, 1977.

———. *Notice to Broadcasters: Federal General Elections: CRTC Guidelines.* Canadian Radio-Television and Telecommunications Commission, Ottawa, 2 February 1978.

———. *CRTC Circular 251.* Canadian Radio-Television and Telecommunications Commission, Ottawa, May 1979.

———. *Broadcasting Guidelines: Federal General Elections.* Canadian Radio-Television and Telecommunications Commission, Circular No. 157, Ottawa, 18 February 1980.

———. *Report of the Royal Commission on Newspapers.* Ottawa: Minister of Supply and Services, 1981.

———. *Report of the Federal Cultural Policy Review Committee.* Ottawa: Supply and Services Canada, 1982.

CANADIAN PRESS ASSOCIATION. *History of Canadian Journalism, I.* Toronto: Canadian Press Association, 1908.

CARELESS, J.M.S. "'Limited Identities' in Canada" *Canadian Historical Review,* 50 (1969), 1-10.

CLARKE, Harold D., et al. *Political Choice in Canada.* Toronto: McGraw-Hill Ryerson, 1979.

———. "Change in the Garden: The 1979 Election" Paper presented at the Annual Meeting of the Canadian Political Science Association, Montreal, 1980.

———. "Voting Behaviour and the Outcome of the 1979 Federal Election: The Impact of Leaders and Issues" *Canadian Journal of Political Science* 15 (1982), 517-552.

CLEMENT, Wallace. *The Canadian Corporate Elite: An Analysis of Economic Power.* Toronto: McClelland & Stewart, 1975.

COCKING, Clive. *Following the Leaders: A Media Watcher's Diary of Campaign '79.* Toronto: Doubleday, 1980.

CROUSE, Timothy. *The Boys on the Bus.* New York: Ballantine Books, 1973.

DEUTSCH, Karl W. *Nationalism and Social Communication: An Inquiry into the Foundations of Nationality.* Cambridge: Massachusetts Institute of Technology Press, 1966.

DONNELLY, Michael G. "The Political Ideas of J.W. Dafoe," in J.H. Aitchison, editor, *The Political Process in Canada: Essays in Honour of R. MacGregor Dawson.* Toronto: University of Toronto Press, 1966, pp. 99-117.

DUNN, S. Watson and Arnold M. BARBAN. *Advertising: Its Role in Modern Marketing.* 5th edition. Toronto: Holt, Rinehart & Winston, 1982.

EDMONDS, J. Duncan. "The Situation of Democracy in Canada and America," Proceedings of the Fourth Seminar on Canadian-American Relations. Windsor: Assumption University, 1962.

ELKIN, Frederick. "Communications Media and Identity Formation in Canada," in Benjamin Singer, ed., *Communications in Canadian Society.* Toronto: Copp Clark, 1972.

EMERY, Edwin. *The Press and America.* 3rd edition. Englewood Cliffs: Prentice Hall, 1972.

EMERY, Walter B. *National and International Systems of Broadcasting.* East Lansing, Mich.: Michigan State University Press, 1969.

FLETCHER, Frederick J. "The Mass Media in the 1974 Canadian Election," in Howard R. Penniman, ed., *Canada at the Polls: The General Election of 1974.* Washington: American Enterprise Institute for Public Policy Research, 1975.

———. "Playing the Game: The Mass Media and the 1979 Campaign," in Howard R. Penniman, ed., *Canada at the Polls, 1979 and 1980: A Study of the General Elections.* Washington: American Enterprise Institute for Public Policy Research, 1981.

———. "The Contest for Media Attention: The 1979 and 1980 Federal Election Campaigns" in *Politics and the Media: An Examination of the Issues Raised by the Quebec Referendum and the 1979 and 1980 Federal Elections.* Toronto: Reader's Digest Foundation of Canada, 1981.

———. *The Newspaper and Public Affairs. Volume 7: Research Publications, Royal Commssion on Newspapers.* Ottawa: Ministry of Supply and Services, 1981.

FLETCHER, Frederick J. and Robert J. DRUMMOND. *Canadian Attitude Trends, 1960-1978.* Montreal: Institute for Research on Public Policy, 1979.

FLETCHER, Frederick J. and Daphne F. GOTTLEIB. "The Mass Media and the Political Process," in Michael Whittington and Glen Williams, eds., *Canadian Politics in the 1980s.* Toronto: Methuen, 1981.

GILSDORF, William O. "Getting the Message Across: The Communication Strategy of the Liberal Party in the 1979 and 1980 Canadian Federal Elections," in Liora Salter, ed., *Communication Studies in Canada*. Toronto: Butterworth's, 1981, pp. 52-67.

GRAFSTEIN, Jerry. "The Anatomy of a Campaign: The Federal Election and the Referendum, or Who Manages Whom?" in *Politics and the Media*. Reader's Digest Foundation, 1981, pp. 66-76.

GRAY, John. "More U.S. Shows, Satellite TV Dishes get Ottawa's Nod," The *Globe and Mail*. 2 March 1983, pp. 1-2.

GREENBERG, B.S. "Person-to-Person Communication in the Diffusion of News Events" *Journalism Quarterly*, 41(1969), 437-40.

HALBERSTAM, David. *The Powers That Be*. New York: Dell Publishing, 1980.

HALFORD, Peter et.al. "A Media Tale of Two Cities: Media Coverage of the Quebec Referendum in Montreal and Toronto" *Canadian Journal of Communication* 9 (Autumn 1983), 1-31.

HEAD, Sydney W. *Broadcasting in America: A Survey of Radio and Television*. 3rd edition. Boston: Houghton Mifflin, 1976.

HENNESSY, Bernard. *Public Opinion*. 4th edition. Monterey: Cole's, 1981.

HILL, Robert. "A Note on Newspaper Patronage in Canada During the Late 1850s and Early 1860s." *Canadian Historical Review*, 49(1968), 44-59.

HOCKIN, Thomas A., ed. *Apex of Power: Prime Minister and Political Leadership in Canada*. Toronto: Prentice-Hall, 1971.

HOLSTI, Ole. *Content Analysis for the Social Sciences and Humanities*. Reading, Mass: Addison-Wesley, 1969.

IRVING, John A. "Interpretations of the Social Credit Movement," in Hugh Thorburn, editor, *Party Politics in Canada*. Toronto: Prentice-Hall, 1963, pp. 85-95.

JANOWITZ, Morris and Paul HIRSCH, eds. *Reader in Public Opinion and Mass Communication*. 3rd edition. New York: Free Press, 1981.

KATZ, Elihu. "The Uses of Becker, Blumler, and Swanson" *Communication Research*, 6(1979), 74-83.

KATZ, Elihu and Paul F. LAZARSFELD. *Personal Influence: The Part Played by People in the Flow of Mass Communications*. New York: Free Press, 1955.

KESTERTON, Wilfred H. *A History of Journalism in Canada*. Toronto: McClelland and Stewart, 1967.

KEY, V.O. Jr. *Public Opinions and American Democracy*. New York: Alfred A. Knopf, 1967.

KLAPPER, Joseph T. *The Effects of Mass Communication*. New York: Free Press, 1960.

KRAUS, Sidney, ed. *The Great Debates: Background, Perspectives, Effects*. Bloomington: Indiana University Press, 1962.

———, ed. *The Great Debates: Carter vs. Ford, 1976*. Bloomington: Indiana University Press, 1979.

KUBAS, Leonard. *Report of the Royal Commission on Newspapers: Volume I, Newspapers and Their Readers*. Ottawa: Ministry of Supply and Services, 1981.

LASSWELL, Harold D. "The Structure and Function of Communication in Society," in L. Bryson, ed., *The Communication of Ideas*. New York: Harper and Brothers, 1948.

LESUEUR, W.S. "The Newspaper Press and the University" *Journalism and the University*. Toronto: Queen's Quarterly, 1903.

LEWIN, Kurt. "Psychological Ecology," in Dorwin Cartwright, ed., *Field Theory in the Social Sciences*. New York: Harper & Bros., 1951.

LEWIS, Flora. "Polls Finally Benefit Voters," Windsor *Star*, March 21, 1983, p. A-10.

LOWER, Arthur R.M. *Colony to Nation: A History of Canada.* Toronto: McClelland & Stewart, 1977.

M'BOW, Amadou-Mahtar. *UNESCO and the Solidarity of Nations: Building the Future.* Paris: The UNESCO Press, 1980.

MCCAIN, Thomas A., Joseph CHILBERG, and Jacob WAKSHLAG. "The Effect of Camera Angle on Source Creditability and Attraction" *Journal of Broadcasting,* 21 (1977), 35-46.

MCDOWELL, Duncan, ed. *Advocacy Advertising: Propaganda or Democratic Right? A Report from the Public Affairs Research Division of the Conference Board of Canada.* Ottawa: Conference Board of Canada, 1982.

MCGINNISS, Joseph. *The Selling of the President.* New York: Trident Press, 1969.

MCLUHAN, Marshall. *Understanding Media.* 2nd edition. New York: Signet Books, 1964.

MEISEL, John. "Formulation of Liberal and Conservative Programs in the 1957 Canadian General Election" *Canadian Journal of Economics and Political Science,* 26 (1960), 565-574.

———. *The Canadian Election of 1957.* Toronto: University of Toronto Press, 1962.

———, ed. *Papers on the 1962 Election.* Toronto: University of Toronto Press, 1964.

———. *Working Papers on Canadian Politics.* 2nd edition. Montreal: McGill-Queen's University Press, 1975.

METALLINOS, Nikos and Robert K. TIEMENS. "Assumptions of the Screen: The Effect of Left Versus Right Placement of Television Images" *Journal of Broadcasting,* 21 (1977) 21-33.

O'BRIEN, John Egli. *A History of the Canadian Radio League: 1930-1936.* Ph.D. dissertation, University of Southern California, 1964.

ONTARIO EDUCATIONAL COMMUNICATIONS AUTHORITY (TVO). "Quartets: Advertising." Four telecasts in February 1982.

PALETZ, David L. and Robert M. ENTMAN. *Media Power Politics.* London: Collier Macmillan, 1981.

PEERS, Frank W. *The Politics of Canadian Broadcasting 1920-1951.* Toronto: University of Toronto Press, 1969.

———. *The Public Eye: Television and the Politics of Canadian Broadcasting, 1952-1968.* Toronto: University of Toronto Press, 1979.

PERRY, Robert L. "Industrial Gaps Left as U.S. Withdraws" *Financial Post,* 25 April 1981, p. 20.

PORAT, Marc V. "Communication Policy in an Information Society," in Glen O. Robinson, ed., *Communications for Tomorrow: Policy Perspectives in the 1980s.* Toronto: Praeger, 1978, pp. 3-60.

PORTER, John. *The Vertical Mosaic: An Analysis of Social Class and Power in Canada.* Toronto: University of Toronto Press, 1965.

POSTMAN, Neil. "The First Curriculum: Comparing School and Television" *Phi Delta Kappan,* 60 (1979), 163-168.

READERS DIGEST FOUNDATION. *Politics and the Media: An Examination of the Issues Raised by the Quebec Referendum and the May 1979 and 1980 Federal Elections.* Toronto, 1981.

REGENSTRIEF, Peter. "The Canadian General Election of 1958" *Western Political Quarterly,* 13 (1960), 349-373.

ROMANOW, Walter I. "The Study of Gatekeepers in Mass Media: A Stance for the Mass Media Critic." Unpublished Paper, University of Windsor, 1973.

ROMANOW, Walter I and Walter C. SODERLUND. "The Southam Press Acquisition of The Windsor Star: A Canadian Case Study of Change" *Gazette: International Journal for Mass Communication Studies,* 24 (1978), 255-270.

ROMANOW, Walter I., W. C. SODERLUND, R. H. WAGENBERG, and E. D. BRIGGS. "Correlates of Newspaper Coverage of the 1979 Canadian Election: Chain-Ownership, Competitiveness of Market, and Circulation." Appendix III to Frederick Fletcher, *The Newspaper and Public Affairs.*

ROPER, Burns W. *An Extended View of Public Attitudes Toward Television and Other Mass Media 1959-1971.* New York: Television Information Office, 1971.

RUTHERFORD, Paul. "The People's Press: The Emergence of the New Journalism in Canada, 1869-99" *Canadian Historical Review,* 56 (1975), 167-191.

———. *The Making of the Canadian Media.* Toronto: McGraw-Hill Ryerson, 1978.

SCARROW, Howard A. "Patterns of Voter Turnout in Canada" *Midwest Journal of Political Science,* 5 (1961), 352-64.

SCHRAMM, Wilbur. "The Gatekeeper: A Memorandum," in Wilber Schramm, ed., *Mass Communications.* Urbana: University of Illinois Press, 1972.

SCHRAMM, Wilbur and William E. PORTER. *Men, Women, Messages and Media.* New York: Harper and Row, 1982.

SEARS, David O., and Steven H. CHAFFEE. "Uses and Effects of the 1976 Debates: An Overview of Empirical Studies," in Sydney Kraus, ed., *The Great Debates: Carter vs. Ford, 1976.* Bloomington, Ind.: Indiana University Press, 1979.

SHAW, Donald L. and Maxwell E. MCCOMBS. *The Emergence of American Political Issues: The Agenda-Setting Function of the Press.* St. Paul: West Publishing Co., 1977.

SIEBERT, Frederick S., Theodore PETERSON, and Wilbur SCHRAMM. *Four Theories of the Press.* Urbana: Illinois University Press, 1973.

SIEGEL, Arthur. *Canadian Newspaper Coverage of the FLQ Crisis: A Study of the Impact of the Press on Politics.* Ph.D. Thesis, McGill University, 1974.

———. *Politics and the Media in Canada.* Toronto: McGraw-Hill Ryerson, 1983.

———. "French and English Broadcasting in Canada - A Political Evaluation" *Canadian Journal of Communications,* 5 (1979), 1-17.

SIMEON, Richard. "Some Suggestions for Improving Intergovernmental Relations," in Paul Fox, ed., *Politics: Canada.* 5th edition. Toronto: McGraw-Hill Ryerson, 1982, pp. 98-102.

SMITH, Denis. "President and Parliament: The Transformation of Parliamentary Government in Canada," in Thomas A. Hockin, ed., *Apex of Power: Prime Minister and Political Leadership in Canada.* Toronto: Prentice-Hall, 1971.

SODERLUND, Walter C. and Ronald H. WAGENBERG. "A Content Analysis of Editorial Coverage of the 1972 Election Campaigns in Canada and the United States" *Western Political Quarterly,* 28 (1975), 335-360.

———. "The Editor and External Affairs: The 1972 and 1974 Election Campaigns" *International Journal,* 31 (1976), 244-54.

SODERLUND, Walter C., et al. "Newspaper Coverage of the 1979 Canadian Federal Election: The Impact of Region, Language, and Chain-Ownership" Paper presented at the Annual Meeting of the Canadian Communication Association, Halifax, 1981.

———. "Regional and Linguistic Agenda Setting in Canada: A Study of Newspaper Coverage of Issues Affecting Political Interpretation in 1976" *Canadian Journal of Political Science,* 13 (1980), 347-56.

SPRY, Graham. "A Case for Nationalized Broadcasting" *Queen's Quarterly,* 38 (1931), 151-169.

STEIN, Robert. *Media Power: Who is Shaping Your Picture of the World?* Boston: Houghton Mifflin, 1972.

STEWART, Andrew. Address to the Canadian Club of Ottawa, 18 April 1962.
——. Address to the Annual Meeting of the Canadian Association of Broad-casters, 3 May 1963.
THONSSEN, Lester, A. Craig BAIRD, and Waldo W. BRADEN. *Speech Criticism.* New York: Ronald Press, 1970.
TROHLDAHL, V. C. "A Field Test of a Modified 'Two-Step Flow of Communications' Model" *Public Opinion Quarterly,* 30 (1966-67), 609-623.
UNESCO. *The Experimental World Literary Programme: A Critical Assessment.* Paris: The UNESCO Press, 1976.
——. *Statistical Reports and Studies: Statistics of Educational Attainment and Literacy, 1945-1974.* Paris: The UNESCO Press, 1977.
——. *Many Voices, One World: Report of the International Commission for the Study of Communication Problems.* New York: United Nations, 1980.
WAGENBERG, Ronald H. and Walter C. SODERLUND. "The Effects of Chain Ownership on Editorial Coverage. The Case of the 1974 Canadian Federal Election" *Canadian Journal of Political Science,* 9 (1976), 683-89.
——. "The Influence of Chain Ownership on Editorial Comment in Canada" *Journalism Quarterly,* 52 (1975), 93-98.
WAGENBERG, Ronald H., et al. "Media Agenda-Setting in the 1979 Canadian Federal Elections: Some Implications for Political Support," in Allan Kornberg and Harold D. Clarke, eds., *Political Support in Canada: The Crisis Years.* Durham: Duke University Press, 1983.
WAITE, Peter B. *The Life and Times of Confederation: Politics, Newspapers, and the Union of British North America.* Toronto: University of Toronto Press, 1967.
WALLACE, Leslie. *Seminar: Advocacy Advertising.* Ottawa: Canadian Radio-television Commission, 1977.
WARD, Norman. "The Press and the Patronage: An Exploratory Operation," in J.H. Aitchison, ed., *The Political Process in Canada: Essays in Honour of R. MacGregor Dawson.* Toronto: University of Toronto Press, 1966, pp. 3-16.
WEEKS, Lewis E. "The Radio Election of 1924" *Journal of Broadcasting,* 8 (1964), 233-43.
WEIR, Ernest A. *The Struggle for National Broadcasting in Canada.* Toronto: McClelland and Stewart, 1965.
WESTELL, Anthony. "The Press: Adversary or Channel of Communication?" in Harold D. Clarke, Colin Campbell, F.Q. Quo, and Arthur Goddard, eds., *Parliament, Policy and Representation.* Toronto: Methuen, 1980.
WHITE, David Manning. "The Gatekeeper: A Study in the Selection of News" *Journalism Quarterly,* 27 (1950), 383-390.
WHITE, Theodore. *The Making of the President, 1960.* New York: Atheneum, 1961.
WHITE, Walter L., Ronald WAGENBERG, and Ralph NELSON. *Introduction to Canadian Politics and Government.* 3rd edition. Toronto: Holt, Rinehart and Winston, 1981.
WILSON, R. Jeremy. "Media Coverage of Canadian Election Campaigns: Horse-race Journalism and the Meta-Campaign" *Journal of Canadian Studies,* 15 (1980-81), 56-68.
WRONG, Denis H. "The Pattern of Party Voting in Canada" *Public Opinion Quarterly,* 21 (1957), 252-64.

Index